MW01235817

REJOICE: A Celebration of Life

Daily Meditations

Written by

Renee Lindsay-Thompson

Book Cover: Artistically Created by Anthony
Garvin of AnthonyGarvinArt
Stone Mountain, GA
www.anthonygarvinart.com

Published by Minister Dr. Jackie S. Henderson
Your Family Research & Publishing
Stone Mountain, GA

To
James ~ Angela,

Keep The Faith!

Love,
Cuz Ronnie

Daily Meditations

Copyright 2012 by Renee Lindsay-Thompson

ISBN-13: 978-1481015936
ISBN-10: 1481015931
Printed in the United States of America

YOUR FAMILY RESEARCH & PUBLISHING

Stone Mountain, Georgia

Dedication

I would like to first thank God who is the head of my life for giving me the vision, strength and inspiration to write this book. It could not have been written without Him. I give God all the glory and honor. I also would like to thank my mother for inspiring me and being the wind beneath my wings, Minister William Richardson for his encouragement and support, Cousin Gina for believing in me, my Sis in Christ Delorise McDuffie and my daughter Lindsay for keeping the ministry going when I could not be there. If we just step out on faith, God will send us the help we need to get the job done. Praise God!

Preface

In everybody's life some rain will fall and what remains after the rain depends on how well we dance through the rain. If we are able to dance through the rain, we can come out of the rain stronger, wiser with more courage, patience, and most of all the victory over our circumstances.

Faced with many trials and tribulations in my life I learned how to dance through the rain with faith, hope and serenity by my side. I fought breast cancer, mastectomy and I am still fighting Fibromyalgia, RSD, loss of career, home foreclosure, marriage difficulties, anxiety and depression.

Even though I am still faced with many trials and tribulations I am still able to dance because I keep my body, soul, and spirit anchored in Christ Jesus by reading the Scriptures and daily mediations I wrote in Rejoice: A Celebration of Life Daily Meditations.

I first started writing the daily meditations in this book to help my family and friends overcome some of the crisis they were facing but then I realized that, the meditations were helping me to make it through the rain. The meditations helped me to understand that with Christ Jesus we can make it through anything and everything that comes our way.

They allowed me to see that everyday we have small victories in our daily life that carry us to the big victories. The small victories are the ones that give us strength to take another step and perseverance to face tomorrow. The small victories we have everyday in our life are the ones where we hold on to the faith we profess, continue to believe and have hope in Christ Jesus despite our circumstances, and when we resist the devil so he can flee.

When we have these small victories we gain the power, faith, hope and serenity that we need to stand firm and never let go. Let us forge ahead by keeping our eyes on the prize, which is Christ Jesus. Amen!

HAVE YOU EVER SAID "GOOD MORNING" TO THE MORNING?

Inspirational poem
by Reverend Lillian Brown-Gold

Take a deep breath
Taste the fresh air,
That's the morning, that's the morning.
Feel your body wrapped in the cool breeze
That's the morning, that's the morning
Hear the birds singing in the trees,
That's the morning, that's the morning.
See the sun a ball of fire rising out of the sky,
That's the morning, that's the morning.
Like strikes of lightening airplanes and cars hurry by,
To catch the morning, catch the morning.
Say "Good morning, morning!"
Thank God for waking me up this morning.
Praise God in the morning.

CONTENTS

DAY I

"But blessed is the man who trusts in the Lord, whose confidence is in him. He will be like a tree planted by the water that sends out its roots by the stream. It does not fear when heat comes; its leaves are always green. It has no worries in a year of drought and never fails to bear fruit."

Jeremiah 17:7-8 NIV

Praise God! Let us put our trust in the Lord and be blessed! The Lord never said life would be without any troubles. However, if we trust in the Lord we can flourish in times of trouble with love, joy and peace, and handle the storms of life without any worries.

Let us know that the Lord will see us through the pouring rain, floods and tornado winds of life. For the battle is mine, says the Lord. Stand firm, have faith and be blessed. Hallelujah! Rejoice in the Lord Always!!

DAY 2

"For this is what the Lord says -- he who created the heavens, he is God; he who fashioned and made the earth, he founded it; he did not create it to be empty, but formed it to be inhabited -- he says: I am the Lord, and there is no other. I have not spoken in secret, from somewhere in a land of darkness; I have not said to Jacob's descendants, Seek me in vain. I, the Lord, speak the truth; I declare what is right."

Isaiah 45:18-19 NIV

Praise God the creator of the heavens and earth from whom all blessings flow! There is no other God like the one we serve. We serve an awesome God who speaks the truth.

God says what He means and means what He says. We can rely on every word of God. Let us not lean on our own understanding, but on every word of God.

Seek God; invite Him into our hearts so we too can declare what is right. Once you invite Him in, He will never leave. God has the whole world in His hands; He has you and me in His hands. Amen! Rejoice in the Lord Always!!

DAY 3

"I urge you, brothers and sisters, to watch out for those who cause divisions and put obstacles in your way that are contrary to the teaching you have learned. Keep away from them. For such people are not serving our Lord Christ, but their own appetites. By smooth talk and flattery they deceive the minds of naive people."

Romans 16:17-18 NIV

Satan has his army out there in the world ready and willing to stop God's plans. Satan does not want any of God's plans to succeed. Satan does not want us to follow, trust, love, worship or praise God. Therefore, let us be alert and not naïve to our surroundings.

Let us pray to God so we can know what His good and perfect will is for us. Everything is not of God or from God. People will say "this is God's will," but in order to know for sure, we must go to the source for ourselves. It's alright to question God if we are not sure. It's better than being deceived. Rebuke Satan in the name of Jesus.

Tell Satan he is a liar and he has no place around here. Also, tell him he cannot have our family or us because we are children of the Almighty God and we choose to serve the Lord. Amen! Hallelujah!! Rejoice in the Lord Always!!

3

DAY 4

"Do not take revenge, my dear friends, but leave room for God's wrath, for it is written: 'It is mine to avenge; I will repay,' says the Lord."

Romans 12:19 NIV

Evilness is all around us and we will encounter it sometimes on a daily basis. However, let us know that God is Mighty and Powerful. He will protect and fight for us.

We don't have to repay evil with evil, but fight evil with prayers. Pray for those who curse and harm us. God knows when and how to make our enemies fall. God will strike them where it hurts the most (better than what we can do).

When we repay evil with evil, we jump from God's side to their side. Let us stay blessed and leave room for God's wrath, not ours. Amen! Praise God! Rejoice in the Lord Always!

DAY 5

"Being confident of this very thing, that he which hath begun a good work in you will perform it until the day of Jesus Christ"

Philippians 1:6 KJV

God did not bring us this far to leave us now. God will complete every project He starts. In order for God's great plans to take effect, sometimes we have to go through some stuff. God has to prepare us for the life He has for us. Therefore, as we go through the storms of life, know that God is preparing us for a blessing; something bigger and better. So let us continue to hold on and have faith in God because He is working out everything according to His plans and our good.

We will come out of the storm better then we went in. We will not be a victim, but a victor with a testimony. Amen! Praise God! Rejoice in the Lord Always!

DAY 6

"Because he loves me," says the Lord, "I will rescue him; I will protect him, for he acknowledges my name. He will call upon me, and I will answer him; I will be with him in trouble, I will deliver him and honor him. With long life I will satisfy him, and show him my salvation."

Psalm 91:14-16 NIV

We serve an awesome God. God will always be there for those who love Him. God will bless, protect, honor, deliver, answer prayers and give salvation to those who seek Him with all their heart, mind and soul.

God first loved us. He gave us His only begotten Son so let us return the love. Love covers a multitude of sins and love never fails. Love the Lord our God with all of our heart, mind and soul. Amen! Praise God! Rejoice in the Lord Always!

DAY 7

"Cast your cares on the Lord and He will sustain you; He will never let the righteous fall."

Psalm 55:22 NIV

God knows all about the hurt, pain, trials and tribulations that are hindering us from enjoying life to the fullest. Let us know that God is here for us. He wants us to give Him all of our cares in prayer.

God does not want that heavy baggage to weigh us down any more. As we give our cares to God, let us leave them with Him and not pick them back up. If we let go and let God, He will erase the pain and mend our broken hearts. We will have joy and peace,

6

instead of pain so that we can rejoice and celebrate the life the Lord has planned in us.

Let us trust God to take away the pain and give us joy. Amen! Praise God! Rejoice in the Lord Always!

DAY 8

"So we fix our eyes not on what is seen, but on what is unseen. For what is seen is temporary, but what is unseen is eternal."
2 Corinthians 4:18 NIV

Our problems don't last forever. Joy comes in the morning. However if we keep focusing on our troubles, we will become depressed, stressed and hopeless. Bigger problems will develop.

Therefore, let us know and believe that God will be with us eternally. He promises to deliver us from all our troubles and give us peace that transcends all understanding.

Let us keep our mind stayed on the Lord so we can rise above any given situation. Amen! Praise God! Rejoice in the Lord Always!

DAY 9

"For there is no difference between Jew and Gentile—the same Lord is Lord of all and richly blesses all who call on Him."
Romans 10:12 NIV

We are children of the Most High and God loves us all the same. Let us call on the name Jesus and something will change. There is power in the name Jesus!! There is healing working power, saving working power, deliverance working power, and hope working power.

When life seems too hard to bear, call on Jesus. He's always near. When we do not know which way to turn, call on Jesus. He knows how to work it out. We can depend on Jesus even when no one else is there. There is power in the name Jesus!!

Call on the name Jesus to get rid of all worries and cares. What a friend we have in Jesus. He took all our sins to bear. JESUS, JESUS, JESUS!! Blessed is he that calls on the name of the Lord. Amen! Praise God! Rejoice in the Lord Always!

DAY 10

"Therefore everyone who hears these words of mine and puts them into practice is like a wise man who built his house on the rock. The rain came down, the streams rose, and the winds blew and beat against that house; yet it did not fall, because it had its foundation on the rock."

Matthew 7:24-25 NIV

We are always either getting ready to go into a storm, in a storm, or coming out of a storm. We need God and the Word of God to help us build a strong foundation so we can withstand the storm and the winds from the storm. God's Word is the truth; it gives us hope, strength and guidance.

Jesus is our Rock in which we stand; all other ground is sinking sand. Let us be obedient to the word of God so our house can stand. Amen! Praise God! Rejoice in the Lord Always!

DAY II

"This, then, is how you should pray: "Our Father in heaven, hallowed be your name, your kingdom come, Your will be done on earth as it is in heaven, give us today our daily bread. Forgive us our debts, as we also have forgiven our debtors. And lead us not into temptation, but deliver us from the evil one."

Matthew 6:9-13 NIV

Prayer is important; it keeps us in the presence of God. It gives us energy for the battle so we can overcome our three enemies: the world, the flesh, and the devil. We cannot fight the battle alone. We need our sword which is the Word of God.

Let us pray without ceasing, knowing that the road gets rough and the going gets tough. Pray to God for He alone is our sustainer and our provider. Amen! Praise God! Rejoice in the Lord Always!

DAY 12

"If the Lord had not been on our side when men attacked us, when their anger flared against us, they would have swallowed us alive; the flood would have engulfed us, the torrent would have swept over us, the raging waters would have swept us away."
Psalm 124:2-5 NIV

Let us meditate on how the Lord is always there for us, and how He has saved and delivered us through the toughest times in our lives. Let us not lose hope, for God is there during our darkest hours demonstrating His infinite love and power. God is faithful, no matter how bad things get. By our side, He will always remain.

When we feel all alone and no one else is there, let us remember we are always in God's love and care. If it had not been for the Lord on our side ... stay on the Lord's side because He is on our side. Amen! Praise God! Rejoice in the Lord Always!

DAY 13

"He alone is my Rock and my salvation; he is my fortress, I will never be shaken."
Psalm 62:2 NIV

Many trials and tribulations are going to come and try to shake us up and knock us down. However, let us hold on to the hope and faith we profess. Know that God is working out everything according to His will and purpose. God will give us the victory over all our troubles. Only with God can our soul find rest and peace in the midst of the storm.

Let God be our shelter in and out of the storm. Trust God! Hold on and never give up. Keep the faith! Rest in the arms of the Lord and never be shaken. Amen! Praise God! Rejoice in the Lord Always!

DAY 14

"Enter His gates with thanksgiving and His courts with praise; give thanks to Him and praise His name."
Psalm 100:4 NIV

Let us praise the Lord from whom all blessings flow. I thank YOU God for your saving grace. We can stand here today with joy in our heart because of all God has done,

12

is doing, and will do for us. Be thankful because He did not have to do it, but He did. God sacrificed His only begotten Son so that we may live life eternally and abundantly.

Let us lift up our holy hands and praise the Lord. As praises go up, blessings come down. Tell the Lord how much we love and appreciate Him. Bless His holy name! Amen! Hallelujah! Rejoice in the Lord Always!

DAY 15

"Come near to God and he will come near to you."
James 4:8 NIV

God does not force himself on us. We are given free will to choose Jesus Christ as our Lord and Savior. We can decide how much we want to know about Christ and how close of a relationship we want to have. When we decide to open up and give our heart to Christ, He will be right there and will never leave us.

Life will never be the same, more blessings, more prayers answered, more success and prosperity. The more we talk to God, rely on Him, and obey His commands, the stronger the bond between Christ and us.

God is at the door knocking and is waiting to come in. Let us open the door and receive Him. If we don't open the door for Christ, Satan will keep occupying that space. Come near to God and receive a new lease on life. Amen! Praise God! Rejoice in the Lord Always!

DAY 16

"Stand firm and you will see the deliverance the Lord will bring you today. The Lord will fight for you; you need only to be still."
Exodus 14:13B, 14 NIV

We are always too busy roaming around doing this and doing that, and forgetting to see God and what He is doing for us and through us.

If we stop trying to do everything ourselves, we will then see the great things the Lord will do for us and through us. Let us be still and know that He is God. God is great, mighty and powerful. He can do everything but fail. The battles we face daily can only be won through the grace of God.

Let us stand firm and wait upon the Lord, then we can see how He will rescue us and deliver us from all of the problems we face. The battle is not ours, it's the Lord's. Stand

and trust the Lord! Amen! Praise God! Rejoice in the Lord Always!

DAY 17

"And Jesus said to them, "I am the bread of life. He who comes to Me shall never hunger, and he who believes in Me shall never thirst."
John 6:35 NKJV

We can eat all day long, but if we don't eat the right foods with the right nutrients, our body won't grow. Sometimes we eat and never get satisfied. Our soul and spirit also need the right kind of food to grow and to be satisfied.

Jesus is the true living bread. He is our spiritual food and only He can give life, growth, and satisfy the spirit and soul. Without Jesus feeding our spirit, we will be walking around with spiritual hunger and deficiency.

Let us feed off Jesus daily through prayer, meditation and reading the Word. When our spirit is fed the right nutrients, we can be strong in the Lord and stand firm in the midst of trouble. Let us hunger and thirst for righteousness and share our bread with others. Amen! Praise God! Rejoice in the Lord Always!

DAY 18

"For all have sinned and fall short of the glory of God."

Romans 3:23 NKJV

No one is immune from committing sins. I don't care how religious we are or how holy we think we are, we still sin. We sometimes sin unknowingly. Some sins are worst then others, but to God a sin is a sin. Therefore, let us come before the Lord's throne of grace daily and pray for forgiveness of our sins.

Our sins separate us from the love of God and forgiveness bridges the gap. God will forgive our sins no matter how big or small and throw them in the sea of forgiveness for them to be heard of no more.

As God forgives us, let us also forgive others and ourselves. "We fall down, but we get up. For a saint is just a sinner who fell down, but we couldn't stay there and got up."* Let us not stay down but get back up again! There is no sin God won't forgive. Know by faith that our sins are forgiven. Amen! Praise God! Rejoice in the Lord Always!

* "We Fall Down" by Donnie McClurkin

DAY 19

"Grace be with you all."
Titus 3:15 NKJV

God's grace is sufficient for us! God's grace brought us this far and it will take us further. God knows how much grace we need and when we need it. By God's grace, we are here today. Grace is the power of God to do for us what we cannot do for ourselves. It is getting the good from God that we do not deserve.

We need God's grace in order to live a joyful, successful, and prosperous life. If it had not been for the grace of God, we don't know where we would be. Let us thank God for His grace. Amen! Praise God! Rejoice in the Lord Always!

DAY 20

"And Peter answered Him and said, "Lord, if it is You, command me to come to You on the water." So, He said, "Come." And when Peter had come down out of the boat, he walked on the water to go to Jesus. But when he saw that the wind was boisterous, he was afraid; and beginning to sink he cried out, saying, "Lord save me!" And immediately Jesus stretched out His hand and caught him, and said to him,"O you of little faith, why did you doubt?"

Matthew 14:28-31 NKJV

With certainty and confidence in Jesus and His power, Peter began to walk on water. However, when Peter took his mind off Jesus and put it on the trouble around him, he began to sink. As Peter was sinking and became afraid, he called out to Jesus realizing it was only He who could save him. When we let the Lord lead us, we are guaranteed to reach our destination. Let us walk by faith, not by sight.

If we keep our mind on the Lord, we won't have the time to worry about our problems. Never doubt God! Amen! Praise God! Rejoice in the Lord Always!

DAY 21

"Wait on the Lord; be of good courage, and He shall strengthen your heart; Wait, I say, on the Lord!"

Psalm 27:14 NKJV

Many of us today hate to wait for anything and anybody. We want everything right now. However, let us remind ourselves that "Haste makes waste" and sometimes we miss our blessing by rushing and being unwilling to wait. Good things do come to those who wait. God wants us to patiently wait on Him for answers and guidance, and not try to handle any situation without Him.

Let us know that God is in control of every situation we face. He knows the urgency, and He knows when to step in and handle it. We miss out on the best way to resolve our situation when we rush and don't wait on the Lord. God is worth waiting for, so let us pray for patience and use the waiting time to renew and refresh our relationship with Him. Amen! Praise God! Rejoice in the Lord Always!

DAY 22

"From the east I summon a bird of prey; from a far-off land, a man to fulfill my purpose. What I have said, that will I bring about; what I have planned, that will I do."

Isaiah 46:11 NIV

God is faithful...we can trust Him at His Word. If God says He is going to do something, believe Him, He will do it. God will not stop until the job is done. God has plans and He will use us to complete them. God just requires us to be humble, ready and willing, and He promises to do the rest. God will give us strength, supply all our needs, and never forsake us. He will give us the victory and endurance to complete the job.

Have faith and know God will do as it is written. God has already done it for Moses, Sarah, Job, Noah and many others. God is faithful even when we are unfaithful. Let us put our faith and trust in God, who never lies or double talks. Amen! Praise God! Rejoice in the Lord Always!

DAY 23

"Love is patient, love is kind. It does not envy, it does not boast, it is not proud. It is not rude, it is not self-seeking, it is not easily angered, it keeps not record of wrongs, love does not delight in evil but rejoices with the truth. It always protects, always trusts, always hopes, always perseveres. Love never fails."

1 Corinthians 13:4-8 NIV

Let true love prevail ... Let us have love for all mankind, even for those who do not love us. Let us pray to God and ask Him to show us the way to love Him, others and ourselves. For only God can show us how to give unselfishly. When we have love, everything else falls into place. Amen! Praise God! Rejoice in the Lord Always!

DAY 24

"What, then shall we say in response to this? If God is for us, who can be against us?"

Romans 8:31 NIV

Without a doubt, God is the greatest of us all. He is stronger, wiser and more knowledgeable than any man is. God is mighty and powerful and He never loses a fight. So let us hang out with the winner because with God, we win. Nothing formed against us shall prevail. God shall shield us from all weapons that come our way to cause us harm or danger. He will then turn around and use those weapons for our good.

With God, we can have the victory over our finances, troubles, enemies, fear, trials and tribulations. If we are on God's side, have no fear; He will always be on our side. Amen! Praise God! Rejoice in the Lord Always!

DAY 25

"Who shall separate us from the love of Christ? Shall trouble or hardship or persecution or famine or nakedness or danger or sword?"

Romans 8:35 NIV

We are going to go through many situations and meet many people that will try to separate us from the love of God. But let us be like Job and hold on to what we know and what God has already done for us. Let us not put our hope and trust in man, material things or Satan, but only in God.

Let our heart stay anchored to Christ, because His love is like no other. The love of

Christ is worth more than gold and more precious than rubies. If we separate ourselves from God, we lose all that God has for us and all that He will do for us. Without the love of Christ, we have nothing. Amen! Praise God! Rejoice in the Lord Always!

DAY 26

"Surely it was for my benefit that I suffered such anguish."
Isaiah 38:17 NIV

Sometimes God will allow not so good things to happen to us. During those times, God has a specific lesson that He wants us to learn. God may want us to call on Him in prayer, draw closer to Him, mature in Christ, or increase our faith. Whatever it is we are going through, let us trust God because He is preparing us for something bigger and better. God has not left us, He is fulfilling His plans. God will see us through the storm.

"It is in the valley where we grow." Let us pray to God and ask Him to help us see the lesson we are to learn. Amen! Hallelujah! Rejoice in the Lord Always!

DAY 27

"Again, the devil took him to a very high mountain and showed him all the kingdoms of the world and their splendor." All this I will give you," he said, "If you will bow down and worship me." Jesus said to him, "Away from me, Satan! For it is written: Worship the Lord your God, and serve him only." Then the devil left him, and angels came and attended him."

Matthew 4:8-11 NIV

Satan is sneaky and cunning. Satan will tempt us with beautiful things or ideas so we can bow down to Him instead of God. Satan will tempt us at our weakest moments which are usually when we are hungry, angry, lonely or tired. However, we can fight back and defeat Satan as Jesus did with the Word of God. The Word of God is powerful, it is our sword and it is the only thing that can defeat Satan.

So let us learn and store the Word of God in our heart to use it when Satan comes our way. Let us tell Satan he is wasting his time because we are not going his way. We serve God and God only. Amen! Praise God! Rejoice in the Lord only!

DAY 28

"But you are a chosen people, a royal priesthood, a holy nation, a people belonging to God, that you may declare the praises of him who called you out of darkness into his wonderful light. For you were like sheep going astray but now you have returned to the Shepherd and Overseer of your souls."

1 Peter 2:9, 25 NIV

Praise God our creator and redeemer...for we were once lost, but now we are found. Let us rejoice, because we belong to God. He has chosen us to be His children and represent Him. We did nothing to deserve such a precious gift. Let us praise God for what He has done and thank Him for His love, grace and mercy. God has given us a new life.

Let us love the Lord with all of our heart and have Faith that His Will will be done in our life. Amen! Praise God! Rejoice in the Lord Always!

DAY 29

"God did extraordinary miracles through Paul, so even handkerchiefs and aprons that had touched him were taken to the sick, and their illnesses were cured and the evil spirits left them."

Acts 19:11-12 NIV

When we give up our own life for the life God has planned for us, He uses us in extraordinary ways. God can use all of us to do great things no matter what we did in our past. Paul called himself the chief of sinners and God used Him. There is something unique and special in all of us that God can use, for we are all fearlessly and wonderfully made. We just have to believe in God and in ourselves.

God does not use us based on our education, how much money we have, where we live, or if we have friends in high places. He uses us based on our willingness to follow and obey Him. If we go to God just as we, He will do the rest. Let us exchange our ordinary life for the extraordinary life God has planned for us. Amen! Praise God! Rejoice in the Lord Always!

DAY 30

"No one can serve two masters. Either he will hate the one and love the other, or he will be devoted to one and despise the other. You cannot serve both God and money."

Matthew 6:24 NIV

Whoever or whatever we concentrate on most will control our thoughts. Money and all our worldly possessions will all fade away and be left behind. 1 Timothy 6:10 says "The love of money is the root of all kinds of evil." Let us choose things that are eternal and never fade away. Let us love God above all things and possessions.

God is our everything. He is all we need. Store up things for heaven, not earth. Amen! Praise God! Rejoice in the Lord Always!

DAY 31

"I can do everything through him who gives me strength."

Philippians 4:13 NIV

God has a life planned for us filled with success and prosperity. And we are going to need a lot of strength in order for God's plan to be fulfilled. However, let us not grow hopeless, weary or tired because we can be successful and prosperous; we can get the job done. Let us know we will not be alone. God will be there with us every step of the way providing the strength we need to overcome any obstacle we may face.

God knows that our natural strength is not strong enough to withstand the turmoil, pressure or the trials and tribulations that may come our way. God's strength is sufficient and with Him, we can accomplish all things. So let us have total reliance on God and not ourselves. Let us not boast about what we can do, but what God can do through us. Have faith and trust in the Lord. Amen! Praise God! Rejoice in the Lord Always!

DAY 32

"The Lord is good, a refuge in times of trouble. He cares for those who trust in him."
Nahum 1:7 NIV

During times of trouble, don't become discouraged and don't let your heart be troubled because God is forever watching over us. We have 24/7 protection with God. He never sleeps nor slumbers, and He knows all about our troubles.

God wants to be our shelter in times of trouble because He loves and cares for us. Therefore, let's seek the Lord in our times of trouble. He will provide all that we need so we can overcome all of our troubles. If God is watching over the birds, bees, animals and fish, let us have faith and know He is watching over us. "His eye is on the Sparrow and I know he watches me."* Let us run to the Lord. He is waiting to shelter us from the storms of life. Amen! Hallelujah! Rejoice in the Lord Always!

*"*His Eye is on the Sparrow*" was originally written in 1905 by lyricist Civilla D. Martin and composer Charles H. Gabriel

DAY 33

"Come now, you who say, "Today or tomorrow we will go to such and such a city, spend a year there, buy and sell, and make a profit"; whereas you do not know what will happen tomorrow. Instead, you ought to say, "If the Lord wills, we shall live and do this or that."

James 4:13-14a,15 NKJV

Let the Lord's will be done, not ours. If we want to make God laugh, make plans. Let us set goals, but know they are subject to change for the better. God is our creator and He already has plans for us so let us allow Him to be the writer, director, manager and producer of every story in our life. God knows how each episode will go and end.

There is nobody more perfect for the job then God. Let us put our life in God's hand. We might not know where we are going, but we know who is directing us. Amen! Praise God! Rejoice in the Lord Always!

DAY 34

"And we know that all things work together for good to those who love God, to those who are the called according to His purpose."
Romans 8:28 NKJV

We know that everything that happens to us will not always be good. And when things go wrong, we get fearful and uncertain about how everything will end. However, let us rejoice because God promises to work all things out for our good. God can turn all of our suffering into something good. He can turn it around so that it works out for our benefit. He will use the suffering to elevate us to a higher level in Him.

This promise can be for us if we accept God, love God, and live according to His will. We can depend on God to do what He says because He is sovereign and has the ability to do all things. God is the key to a more fulfilling and joyful life.

With God, we don't have to be fearful or uncertain because we know how everything will end. Let us love the Lord so we can be called according to His purpose. Let go! Let God! Amen! Praise God! Rejoice in the Lord Always!

DAY 35

"All scripture is God-breathed and is useful for teaching, rebuking, correcting and training in righteousness, so that the man of God may be thoroughly equipped for every good work."

2 Timothy 3:16-17 NIV

Let us not go anywhere without our sword, which is the Word of God. Let us store the Word in our heart and mind. There is power in the Word. We can triumph over the challenges we face in life with the Word. God's Word gives us instructions on how to celebrate life to the fullest. Let us read and know the Bible for ourselves.

God's Word is powerful. It carries a punch. Amen! Praise God! Rejoice in the Lord Always!

DAY 36

*"The Lord will give strength to His people; the
Lord will bless His people with peace."*
Psalm 29:11 NKJV

The Lord will supply all the strength we
need...let us trust Him. The same strength
that God used to raise Christ from the dead
lies within us and is available to us during our
weakest moments. So during our weakest
moments, let us look within ourselves and
know the Lord is there supplying all the
strength we need so we can have victory over
all things that may come our way.

When we trust and have faith in God and
know that He will supply all the strength we
need, we can then find peace in the midst of
our weakest moments. Therefore, when we
need strength; let us rely on the Lord. When
we want triumph over our problems, let us
rely on the Lord; He will give us strength. Let
us have faith and rely on God. Amen! Praise
God! Rejoice in the Lord Always!

DAY 37

"For we do not have a high priest who is unable to sympathize with our weakness, but we have one who has been tempted in every way, just as we are--yet was without sin."
Hebrews 4:15 NIV

Let us not think the Lord does not understand our weakness or the temptations we have to encounter. He does! Our Lord is the Father of Compassion. He beholds empathy and compassion for us and everything we have to go through. For He has encountered the same temptations we are facing today; same temptations, just different era.

So let us not feel ashamed to call on the Lord, pray, or recite scripture for spiritual strength when we are weak from temptation. Jesus did when He was tempted, and He was able to resist the temptation. So let us arm ourselves with spiritual strength and win the war. Amen! Praise God! Rejoice in the Lord Always!

DAY 38

"I took you from the ends of the earth, from its farthest corners I called you. I said, "You are my servant", I chose you and have not rejected you."

Isaiah 41:9 NIV

Let us rejoice and know God has chosen us to help fulfill His purpose here on earth. God gives us visions to carry out His will and purpose. We may feel that we are incapable of fulfilling His will. But let us know, when God gives a vision, He will provide the resources so that His purpose can be fulfilled. He will send people in our lives to encourage, teach and guide us.

We may feel unworthy to do God's will because of past mistakes. God's Word tells us not to focus on our past, but have hope, and continue to ask for the strength and courage to do His will. We may face many distractions along the way, but know that God will bring us through each difficulty to reach another ladder upward towards fulfilling His purpose. Amen! Praise God! Rejoice in the Always!

DAY 39

"Then Jesus told his disciples a parable to show them, that they should always pray and not give up."

Luke 18:1 NIV

Prayer changes things...God is a life changer. Let us keep our prayer requests constantly before God knowing that he will answer them. God will answer our prayers in His time and according to His will, not ours. Let us not give up on prayer because we did not like God's answer or because we felt He took too long to answer. Let us trust God's answers to our prayers because He has our best interest in His heart.

As we constantly pray, we grow in character, faith and hope. Let God's will be done, not ours. Go before God daily in prayer. Amen! Praise God! Rejoice in the Lord Always!

DAY 40

"Oh come, let us sing to the Lord! Let us shout joyfully to the Rock of our salvation. For the Lord is the great God, and the great King above all gods."

Psalm 95:1, 3 NKJV

Praise the Lord! Sing praises to God! He is worthy to be praised. Let us clear our mind from all thoughts that will hinder our praise. Let us rejoice and celebrate God's greatness and all that He has done. Let us be thankful, shout for joy, and have an attitude of gratitude!

We were chosen by God to praise Him and declare His goodness to others. Let praises for the Lord overflow from our heart to our lips for there is no other God like the one we serve. He is the King of Kings and the Lord of Lords. Praise the Lord with the highest praise. Hallelujah! Amen! Praise God! Rejoice in the Lord Always!

DAY 41

"For nothing is impossible with God."
Luke 1:37 NIV

God is still in the miracle making business! We serve the same God that created the heavens and earth, gave sight to the blind, and allowed the cripple to walk. With God, unexplainable things happen. Let us continue to have the faith that God can and will make a way out of no way.

When we've done all we can, let us pray, stand and wait on the Lord. God will show up and show out. Amen! Praise God! Rejoice in the Lord Always!

DAY 42

"Through wisdom a house is built, and by understanding it is established; by knowledge the rooms are filled with all precious and pleasant riches."
Proverbs 24:3-4 NKJV

The foundation of a home is very important. A wise man builds his house on a strong foundation and it stands forever. A house built on shaky ground falls. It's not able to withstand the winds, rain, or floods. Let us be wise and build our life on a strong foundation. A strong foundation is not easily moved and is able to withstand any given situation.

We can have that strong foundation if we build a strong relationship with Christ. God is mighty and power-ful and only He can sustain us. Let God be the Architect we consult. God knows how to build a strong house. He has the blueprints and all the material we need. Amen! Praise God! Rejoice in the Lord Always!

DAY 43

"Your eyes are too pure to look on evil; you cannot tolerate wrong. Why then do you tolerate the treacherous? Why are you silent while the wicked swallow up those more righteous than themselves?"

Habakkuk 1:13 NIV

Habakkuk was asking God how does evil flourish and triumph over the righteous when we serve a just God. I know we all have at times become angry, disgusted and discouraged because we felt evil was going unpunished. God promised Habakkuk that the evil would be punished and not to worry or lose hope. God reassured Habakkuk that He is working everything out according to His plan and in His time.

Let us wait and trust God even when we do not understand the events that are occurring. God hates sin and He has everything under His control. God is not silent. He will prevail, not evil! Evil is self-destructive, because they trust in Satan, themselves and not God. Amen! Praise God! Rejoice in the Lord Always!

DAY 44

"From the fullness of his grace we have all received one blessing after another."
                                        John 1:16 NIV

We did nothing and we can't do nothing to earn or deserve God's grace. Grace is unmerited favor from God. God chooses to bless us everyday because of his goodness and love for us. However, sometimes we miss or don't recognize our own blessings because we believe it's something we did ourselves or it was luck. Everything good and perfect is a blessing from God and not from us or because of luck. God's blessings of grace and mercy bestowed upon us make all things possible.

Let us thank God for the many blessings He has bestowed upon us. By God's amazing grace, we are saved, have eternal life, and have a life that we can rejoice and celebrate. Amen! Praise God! Rejoice in the Lord Always!

DAY 45

"He will feed His flock like a shepherd; he will gather the lambs with his arms, and carry them in His bosom, and gently lead those who are with young."
                                        Isaiah 40:11 KJV

The Lord is our shepherd...we shall not be in want. The Lord is our everything. With so many things going on today, we need God more then ever. The Lord will comfort us in His heavenly arms and give us faith, hope, peace, and joy in the midst of our troubles. Whatever is going on in our life, let us remember God is still with us and He is still in the miracle making business.

With God, we can hold on and stand firm against any problems we may come up against big or small. Let us hold on to God's unchanging hands. Hold on, we can make it...the blessing is at the door! After the rain, the sun will shine! Amen! Praise God! Rejoice in the Lord Always!

DAY 46

"When He finished speaking, He said to Simon, "Put out into the deep water, and let down the nets for a catch." Simon answered, "Master we've worked hard all night and haven't caught anything. But because you say so, I will let down the nets." When they had done so, they caught such a large number of fish that their nets began to break."

Luke 5:4-6 NIV

Many of us find it difficult to obey God. We feel we know more or better than God. We think we can make our own decisions and still succeed. Let us know God is much wiser and knowledgeable then we will ever be. We won't make half of the mistakes we do if we just listen to God.

When we obey God, He opens up the windows of heaven and pours us out a blessing and we will not have enough room to receive it just as he did for Simon.   Amen! Praise God! Rejoice in the Lord Always!

DAY 47

"Yet not what I will, but what you will."
Mark 14:36B NIV

Let us stop complaining about our life and do something about it. God stands here before us with great plans for our life and yet we do not take time to ask or listen to what they are. Let us pray and meditate on the Word of God because we then will find out His great and perfect will is for us.   We would have less stress in our life if we do God's will instead of our own.

God knew us before we were formed in our Mother's womb and he predestined us for greatness. Let us be what God wants us to be. Everything that comes from God is great and perfect. Amen! Praise God! Rejoice in the Lord Always!

DAY 48

"So they called them and commanded them not to speak at all nor teach in the name of Jesus. But Peter and John answered and said to them, "Whether it is right in the sight of God to listen to you more than to God, you judge."

Acts 4:18-19 NKJV

We are to speak boldly about God and win souls for Christ. Tell others what God has done for us and through us so they too may believe. We are reliable witnesses for Christ. Some non-believers are going to tell us to "Be quiet," but we are to listen to God and not man. We never know whose life we will touch and help change forever by the Word of God.

Let us not deny others the chance to live a better life with Christ. Don't spread gossip; spread the "Good News" about Christ! Amen! Praise God! Rejoice in the Lord Always!

DAY 49

"Then the peoples around them set out to discourage the people of Judah and make them afraid to go on building."
Ezra 4:4 NIV

Many times when we are doing something good or trying to better ourselves, negative people will come along and try to knock us down and stop us. If we prayed and our vision is in line with God's vision, then we have nothing to worry about. God will prepare the way for us. God will open doors, give us the qualifications, put the right people in our life to help, and supply all the resources we need.

Yes, we might have some setbacks, but have faith and push forward. Let us not allow the naysayers to derail us and steal our blessing. Amen! Praise God! Rejoice in the Lord Always!

DAY 50

"I am the Lord your God; consecrate yourselves and be holy, because I AM Holy."
Leviticus 11:44 NIV

Let us be an imitator of God and follow in his ways. To be holy does not mean we are a geek, unfashionable, corny or better than others. It means we are following in the ways of the Lord. In other words, trying to walk right, talk right, and do right so we can be alright. Life is much better when we follow in the ways of the Lord.

The flesh is weak and we need the strength of the Lord in order to live right. We will never be perfect, but we can strive toward the prize. Amen! Praise God! Rejoice in the Lord Always!

DAY 51

"Do not fret because of evil men or be envious of those who do wrong. Trust in the Lord and do good; dwell in the land and enjoy safe pasture."

Psalm 37:1,3 NIV

Sometimes it might be easy for us to envy the wicked and fall prey to doing wrong. Especially, when we see a schemer or shyster doing well and getting what we want. However, let us never envy the wicked for what they have is not God given and it might not last a lifetime.

We can't ever beat God's giving. God gives us what we need and some of our wants. If God didn't give it to us, it means we do not need it like we think. God knows what we need before we do. What God gives us will last forever. God is our key to happiness and not material possessions or money. Amen! Praise God! Rejoice in the Lord Always!

DAY 52

"Taste and see that the Lord is good; blessed is the man who takes refuge in Him."
Psalm 34:8 NIV

God is good all the time; all the time God is good. There is nobody better to us than God, not even ourselves. God invites us to get to know Him so we can see all of His goodness and build a strong relationship with Him. We will never know how good God is until we get to know Him. When we follow the Lord and take shelter in Him, we will discover His goodness. Let us remember the many blessings God has already bestowed upon us.

Let us focus on God and what He has already done for many others and us. Trust the Lord daily and see how good He is. Amen! Praise God! Rejoice in the Lord Always.

DAY 53

"Each of you should look not only to your own interests, but also to the interests of others."
Philippians 2:4 NIV

On September 11, 2001, many people lost their lives or loved ones, but we came together as a community and a nation. We united in love, helping and caring for each other. This helped many victims and survivors triumph over their circumstances. They were able to endure the pain and find hope.

Let us continue to be our brothers and sisters' keepers. Together with love, we can overcome and conquer the trials and tribulations that come our way. Amen! Praise God! Rejoice in the Lord Always!

DAY 54

"But lift up your rod, and stretch out your hand over the sea and divide it. And the children of Israel shall go on dry ground through the midst of the sea."
Exodus 14:16 NKJV

The Israelites came across many obstacles as Moses led them out of captivity. However, the Lord was right there with them every step of the way, giving them guidance. God equipped Moses with the power to move the obstacles, gave Moses a helper, and provided them with strength, food and faith. We will face many obstacles as we try to release ourselves from the trials and tribulations that are holding us captive. Hallelujah!

We too can break loose with God's help. With a little bit of faith, we can move mountains. God set the Israelites free and He will do the same for us -- success guaranteed. Don't be hopeless let us put our hope in God. Amen! Praise God! Rejoice in the Lord Always!

DAY 55

"Now faith is being sure of what we hope for and certain of what we do not see."
Hebrews 11:1 NIV

How much faith will it take us to follow Christ and literally believe in His word?

We say we have faith, but we sometimes put more faith in man and in ourselves than in God. But God is wiser and He already has our life planned out. So why not have more faith in Him? Putting our faith in God will take us to places we have never seen before and doing things we never thought were possible. We can trust and depend on God; He will never break a promise.

However, we will sometimes let ourselves down and with man, nothing is guaranteed. Let us approach the throne of grace with confidence and certainty, knowing God is who He says He is and He will do what He says. Let us "Live by faith and not by sight." If we take the first step, God will do the rest. Amen! Praise God! Rejoice in the Lord Always!

DAY 56

"The Lord Himself goes before you and will be with you; he will never leave you nor forsake you."

Deuteronomy 31:8 NIV

Let us be encouraged and know our God, our Father, loves us and cares for us His children and He will never leave us. The Lord has brought us from a very long way and He did not bring us this far to leave us. The good works God started in us He will continue for all of eternity. Therefore, let us rejoice and know for sure that the Lord is with us during good or bad, happy or sad situations.

So let us never think the Lord is not around or He has forgotten about us because something bad happened, or something was not done according to our time. In all situations, let us have hope knowing the Lord is near. The Lord will never leave nor forsake us. Amen! Praise God! Rejoice in the Lord Always!

DAY 57

"He found him in a desert land and in the wastelands, a howling wilderness; He encircled him, He instructed him. He kept him as the apple of His eye."
Deuteronomy 32:10 NKJV

We were lost in the darkness of the world when God came and gave us a new life -- a new life filled with love, hope, faith, joy, peace, blessings, grace and mercy.

He showed us how to not only survive, but how to thrive in the midst of the dark cruel world. We no longer have to walk around in the darkness because we walk with the Lord, the light of the world. Let us appreciate what God has done for us. God forgave our past life and gave us a new life. We are new creatures with a renewed heart, soul and spirit.

God loves us, guides us, protects us and sustains us. We are children of the Most High God. Hallelujah! Thank you Lord for saving a wretch like me! If we follow Jesus, the Light of the world, we will never have to walk in darkness again. Amen! Praise God! Rejoice in the Lord Always!

DAY 58

"Therefore do not worry about tomorrow, for tomorrow will worry about its own things. Sufficient for the day is its own trouble."
Matthew 6:34 NKJV

Let us live one day at a time. Planning for the future is good; worrying about the future is a waste of time. God is in control of our life and His "will" will be done no matter what. So, instead of us worrying about the future, let us talk to God and find out what He has planned for our future. We know it is going to be good because He promises to prosper us. We have to learn how to give all of our worries to God in prayer so we can concentrate on accomplishing the goals He has set for us.

If we worry about tomorrow, we hamper our efforts today. Tomorrow will take care of itself. Let us trust and have faith in God. He knows all about our troubles and He will take care of them all. So why worry? Amen! Praise God! Rejoice in the Lord Always!

DAY 59

"When I broke the five loaves for five thousand, how many baskets full of fragments did you take up?" They said to Him "Twelve."
Mark 8:19 NKJV

God can make a way out of no way. Let us have no doubt about what God can do.

Our situation sometimes might seem hopeless, but let us remember we serve an awesome God who can take five loaves of bread and feed thousand and have some left over. So let us have faith in God and know nothing is ever hopeless when we trust God to work it out. We can trust God to bring us through any situation again and again. We might not have the ability to make everything happen, but God does.

God can heal, deliver, bless, and perform miracles...He does everything that is good and perfect. Let us trust God to work out things out for us. Amen! Praise God! Rejoice in the Lord Always!

DAY 60

"As the deer pants for the water brooks, so pants my soul for You, O God. My soul thirsts for God, for the living God."
Psalm 42:1-2a NKJV

We serve the only true living God. Let our soul thirst for Him. The deer depends on water to help them live, especially when hunters are chasing them. As a deer depends on water, let us depend on God to help us live now and for eternity. God promises to help us when the storms, our enemies, trials and tribulations, come.

Let us pray to God and tell Him "I need you now." When we depend on God, we focus our thoughts on His ability and take the focus off our inability. God loves and cares for us. He wants us to trust and depend on Him every day and for all things.

We keep hope alive when we trust and depend on God. Let us stop depending on man and depend on God! Trust God! Amen! Praise God! Rejoice in the Lord Always!

DAY 61

"The Lord is my light and my salvation; whom shall I fear? The Lord is the strength of my life; of whom shall I be afraid?"
Psalm 27:1 NKJV

Fear can be powerful. It can overtake our life and ruin our happiness if we allow it to. God did not give us a spirit of fear. Therefore, our being fearful is not of God. God wants us to live by faith and know for certain that He will be with us as we go through our life journey. With God, we have nothing to fear, because everything in life will turn out the way it should; nothing is going to happen by coincidence.

Satan wants us to live a life of fear and doubt so that we will never succeed or have true happiness with God. Let us have "No Fear," because God has us wrapped up in His everlasting love. He has promised to never leave us no matter where we are or because of what we have done. Let us keep the faith of Moses, Noah and Mary. Amen! Praise God! Rejoice in the Lord Always!

DAY 62

"I remember the days of long ago; I meditate on all your works and consider what your hands have done."

Psalm 143:5 NKJV

Let us meditate on the goodness of the Lord day and night. Let us always remember and never forget what the Lord has done for us. The Lord has been better to us than we have been to ourselves. Nobody can do us like the Lord. God has made a way out of no way and He sustained us through another night. Remembering the goodness of the Lord helps us to remain hopeful in the midst of the storm.

The Lord is always faithful, even when we are not. Thank God and remember His sacrifice, love, blessings, wonderful deeds, healing, comfort, protection, provisions, grace and mercy. God is good all the time and all the time God is good. Amen! Praise God! Rejoice in the Lord Always!

DAY 63

"So he answered and said to me: "This is the word of the Lord to Zerubbabel: 'Not by might, nor by power, but by My Spirit,' says the Lord of hosts."
Zechariah 4:6 NKJV

In our own human power and by our own might, we are limited in what we can do. However, "We can do all things through Christ who strengthens us." We can accomplish many great things when we totally rely on the Spirit of God to help us. When we get tired, weary, and the road gets rough, we can depend on God to give us enough strength so we can continue to push forward and not give up.

Daily Meditations

Let us confess to God that we can't do anything without Him. For it is through His Spirit that we can do all things. Let us totally rely on God for success. He will help us to reach the top. With God, we can make it happen! Amen! Praise God! Rejoice in the Lord Always!

DAY 64

"Yet the Lord longs to be gracious to you; he rises to show you compassion. For the Lord is a God of justice. Blessed are all who wait for him!"

Isaiah 30:18 NIV

God is good, His love endures forever. Sometimes we are going to have what we call "bad days," because something we didn't like happened to us. Either our phone broke, we overslept, our hair does not look right, or somebody said something we didn't like.

During these times, let us stop cursing, complaining and frowning, and remember that the Lord is gracious and compassionate. Know that God is on our side and He can turn bad into good. We make our own days bad and miss our blessing by not waiting for the Lord to work things out.

55

The next time something happens we don't like, let us trust God, keep smiling, and tell Satan we will not get mad. Amen! Praise God! Rejoice in the Lord Always!

DAY 65

"Have I not commanded you? Be strong and courageous. Do not be terrified; do not be discouraged, for the Lord your God will be with you wherever you go."
Joshua 1:9 NIV

We need to have consistent faith and be courageous if we are going to keep living for Christ and doing His will. There are so many obstacles placed in our way when we try to draw closer to God. These obstacles are to discourage and deter us from God's plan for us.

However, we need not to be terrified or get discouraged, because God is with us all the way. Therefore, when we come across our haters and people that are mean, rude and nasty pray and love them, because they are just being used. Let our haters be our motivators.

We have come this far by faith so let us not allow anything or anyone stop us from doing the will of God and block our blessings.

Don't give them that much power. Amen!
Praise God! Rejoice in the Lord Always!

DAY 66

"Then the Lord said to Moses, "Now you will see what I will do to Pharaoh: Because of my mighty hand he will let them go; because of my mighty hand he will drive them out of his country."

Exodus 1:1 NIV

Let us throw "can't" out of our vocabulary and spirit. Through God, we have all the power in our hand and we don't even recognize it. God is all-powerful. When we can't in our natural strength, we can with God. God will give us the power and strength to overcome all our trials and tribulations and succeed in all he calls us to do. God did it for Moses and he will do it for us.

In Exodus 4:21 "The Lord said to Moses, "When you return to Egypt, see that you perform before Pharaoh all the wonders I have given you the power to do."

When the Red Sea had to be parted, God told Moses to stretch out his hand. Let us know "we are more than conquerors." Amen! Praise God! Rejoice in the Lord Always!

DAY 67

"But now the Lord has abandoned us and put us into the hand of Midian."
Judges 6:13c NIV

Let us know God will never abandon us His children. He takes care of us day and night, no matter where we are. He neither sleeps nor slumbers. When we feel God has abandoned us, let us look at ourselves and ask, "Did I abandon God?" We ask ourselves this question because sometimes we will abandon God knowingly and unknowingly with our sins. Our sins separate us from the love of God.

But let us rejoice and know there is a way back into a right relationship with God. We don't have to be separated from God too long. We are reunited with Christ when we have a change of heart and repent for our sins. When we fall, let us get up! God will forgive us! Amen! Praise God! Rejoice in the Lord Always!

DAY 68

"Finally, brethren, whatever things are true, whatever things are noble, whatever things are just, whatever things are pure, whatever things are lovely, whatever things are of good report, if there is any virtue and if there is anything praiseworthy—meditate on these things."

Philippians 4:8 NKJV

We need to be mindful of the things we put in our minds. What we plant in our minds comes out in our words and actions. Then they become our character. A man is what he thinketh. Let us replace negative thoughts with positive ones. If we keep our mind on things which are of God, then the God of peace will be with us and our thoughts will be pure and noble.

Let us allow the words of our mouth and the meditation of our heart be pleasing to God, our Lord and Savior. Amen! Praise God! Rejoice in the Lord Always!

DAY 69

"Trust in the Lord with all your heart, and lean not on your own understanding; in all your ways acknowledge Him, and He shall direct your paths."

Proverbs 3:5-6 NKJV

If we want to make fewer mistakes in life, we should consult God before making any decisions, big or small. Without God, we are limited in our resources and knowledge. God is all knowing. He knows how everything will begin and end. God knows what we need before we do. If we allow God to direct our paths, we can have an abundant life full of blessings, success and prosperity.

Jeremiah 29:11 tells us "For I know the plans I have for you," declares the Lord, "plans to prosper you and not to harm you, plans to give you hope and a future." If we want to reach our destination, let us trust God. Amen! Praise God! Rejoice in the Lord Always!

DAY 70

"For when I am weak, then I am strong."
2 Corinthians 12:10 NIV

There will be circumstances in our life that will make us weak and bring us to our knees. However, let us rejoice and know even though we are weak, we can still make it and have the victory over any circumstance or crisis we may face because the Lord's strength is made perfect in our weakness. When we are weak, the Lord provides us with His strength and then we become stronger than we ever could be on our own.

So when obstacles come in our life, let us depend on the Lord and His strength to see us through. God has an abundance of strength. He never gets tired or weak. When life gets tough, let us know God makes us tough. We can make it with God. Through prayer, let us tap into the source of our strength. Amen! Praise God! Rejoice in the Lord Always!

DAY 71

"And now these three remain: faith, hope and love. But the greatest of these is love."
1 Corinthians 13:13 NIV

If we have not loved, we have profited nothing. The greatest of all human qualities is love and it is an attribute of God. Love is available for everyone and it makes our actions and spiritual gifts useful. After all the things in our life fade away, love will always remain. Let us ask God to set aside our selfish ways so we can be free to love without looking for something in return.

As we grow in the Lord, we can understand how God loves. Let us first love God with all of our heart and soul, and then love thy neighbor as thyself. Let us put love into action. Amen! Praise God! Rejoice in the Lord Always!

DAY 72

"And the apostles said to the Lord, "Increase our faith." So the Lord said, "If you have faith as a mustard seed, you can say to this mulberry tree, 'Be pulled up by the roots and be planted in the sea,' and it would obey you."

Luke 17:5-6 NKJV

The amount of faith is not as important as the right kind of faith. A mustard seed is small, but if we plant it in the right pot and soil, it will take root and grow. The same is with faith. A small amount of genuine faith in God will take root and grow. Our faith will grow as we totally depend on God and do His will.

With prayer and a small amount of genuine faith in God, we can begin to walk by faith and not by sight. Let us have complete genuine faith in God and not in man. Amen! Praise God! Rejoice in the Lord Always!

DAY 73

"God is a consuming fire."
Hebrews 12:29 NKJV

We serve a Great God; Mighty and Powerful. God is able to do everything but fail. God is a raging fire that cannot be contained with human control. He does everything according to His will and in His time. There is nothing too hard for God. God, not man, has the last word in everything. So, let us love, obey and follow God.

For there is no other man or god that can do what He does. He is above all and He is our all in all. He will lead us and show us the right way to go. As children of God, let us have faith, fear and trust in Him forever more. His flame never goes out. God is... and He will... Amen! Praise God! Rejoice in the Lord Always!

DAY 74

"When neither sun nor stars appeared for many days and the storm continued raging, we finally gave up all hope of being saved. But now I urge you to keep up your courage, because not one of you will be lost; only the ship will be destroyed. Last night an angel of the God whose I am and whom I serve stood beside me, and said, 'Do not be afraid, Paul."
Acts 27:20,22-24a NIV

Sometimes it feels like the storm just keeps on raging and it will never end. At those times, some of us become hopeless and feel like God is nowhere to be found. However, let us rejoice in knowing that the sun will shine. Don't be afraid God is always with us, He will never leave us, He knows all about our troubles and He will deliver us from all of our troubles (in His time, not ours).

Therefore, let us hold on to our faith like Job and continue to praise the Lord anyhow. Trouble does not last forever and there is a blessing after the storm. Amen! Praise God! Rejoice in the Lord Always!

DAY 75

"If anyone sees his brother commit a sin that does not lead to death, he should pray and God will give him life."
1 John 5:16 NIV

No matter where we are or where we go, we will not find a perfect person. We will not find them at our place of work, at our home or in our church, for only God in heaven is perfect. Therefore, let's pray and love one another and leave the judgment up to God. We can't talk about another's sin or imperfections when we have our own. We might not commit the same sin, but a sin is a sin. "For the same way we judge others, we too will be judged."

Let us take the plank out of our own eye before we take the sawdust out of someone else's. Prayer and love is the greatest gift we can give to each other. Let us love as God loves us. Amen! Praise God! Rejoice in the Lord Always!

DAY 76

"You are of God, little children, and have overcome them, because He who is in you is greater than he who is in the world."
1 John 4:4 NKJV

Satan is in the world prowling around trying to steal, kill and destroy. However, let us remember we are children of the Most High God who is Mighty and Powerful and there is nobody greater. The Holy Spirit dwells in us forever. He will never leave nor forsake us, and He will comfort, help and rescue us when our hearts are troubled and we cannot pray. If we make the Lord our refuge and fortress and trust in Him, then we can overcome all trouble, illness, and evilness.

There is no sorrow the Lord can't fix. Let us trade in our fear for faith and trust in God. Amen! Praise God! Rejoice in the Lord Always!

DAY 77

"What a heavy burden God has laid on men!"
Ecclesiastes 1:13b NIV

We serve a merciful God who hears us and cares for us day by day. He will never give us more than we can carry or bear. God will neither abandon nor destroy us. If He sends us to it, He will make sure that we will make it through it. So let us look to the hills from which our help comes. The Lord is our help. Only He can sustain and deliver us from all the burdens we bear. Trust the Lord for all our burdens He will bear. Let us free our minds from all worries and cares.

Let us take our burdens to the Lord in prayer. Let us leave them there in the Lord's precious care. If we hold on to the Lord's unchanging hands, there will be no burden too heavy for us to bear. Amen! Praise God! Rejoice in the Lord Always!

DAY 78

"Finally, be strong in the Lord and his mighty power. Put on the full armor of God so that you can take your stand against the devil's schemes."

Ephesians 6:10-11 NIV

We can be sure that anytime we try to get closer to the Lord the devil is going to be mad, show up and be disruptive. Satan has a powerful army and they will try anything to impart negative thoughts and feelings. However, we can be assured of the victory. But until Christ returns, we must engage in this battle. With God's supernatural power, Satan can be defeated.

In order for us to achieve "victory," we must depend on God's strength, pray and make use of every piece of His armor (read vs. 10-20). We can depend on God to see us through. The battle is not ours, it's the Lord's. Amen! Praise God! Rejoice in the Lord Always!

DAY 79

"Look to the Lord and His strength; seek His face always."

1 Chronicles 16:11 NIV

Whatever goes on in our life good or bad, let us look to the Lord always. God's thoughts and ways are higher than ours. Don't let our love for the Lord change with our circumstances. Let us love the Lord with all our heart and soul always. God is always for us, not against us. How we feel about God affects our blessings, serenity and joy. We might feel we have been dealt a bad hand, but don't turn away from God, turn to God.

With God, we can bounce back from any adversity. Don't give up on God. Seek his face always! Amen! Praise God! Rejoice in the Lord Always!

DAY 80

"It is better to trust in the Lord than to put confidence in man."
Psalm 118:8 KJV

If we are going to put our confidence in someone, it might as well be God. God has the proven track record for looking out for our best interests. We know what God can do for us; we have experienced His love, power and goodness. Let us make God the head of our life and let Him guide us daily. God never takes a wrong turn.

When we trust God, we can have that security knowing that we are in the best hands possible. God does not change with the wind, but man does. Amen! Praise God! Rejoice in the Lord Always!

DAY 81

"Where can I go from your Spirit? Where can I flee from your presence? If I go up to the heavens, you are there; if I make my bed in the depths you are there. If I rise on the wings of the dawn, if I settle on the far side of the sea, even there your hand will guide me, your right hand will hold me fast."
Psalm 139:7-10 NIV

God is everywhere we are. We are always in His divine presence. He watches over us day and night. We never have to walk alone or face any crisis alone for God walks with us. So when we are fearful and frightened, let us look up and know God is near.

We are God's children. He loves us and does not want any harm or danger to come to us. He watches over us as He watches over the sparrow. Amen! Praise God! Rejoice in the Lord Always!

DAY 82

"Not that I speak in regard to need, for I have learned in whatever state I am, to be content."

Philippians 4:11 NKJV

It is hard for us to be content in all circumstances because the flesh always wants more. Our spirit can be content but our flesh is rarely ever satisfied. So until Jesus Christ comes again our spirit and our flesh will continue to battle with our spirit wanting to do the will of God and our flesh wanting to do the will of the world. But let us know if we keep our mind on the Lord, pray for patience and remember the Lord is not done with us yet. He has more blessings coming our way.

Our spirit can win the battle over the flesh and we can learn how to be content in all circumstances. Let us stand firm, be content, and wait on the Lord to give us what He has for us because what He has for us is for us, and nobody can take that away. Amen! Praise God! Rejoice in the Lord Always!

DAY 83

"And when He got into the boat, he who had been demon-possessed begged Him that he might be with Him. However, Jesus did not permit him, but said to him, "Go home to your friends, and tell them what great things the Lord has done to you, and how He has had compassion on you."
Mark 5:18-19 NKJV

"Now run and tell that!" Everyone seems to be in such a hurry to run spread gossip. How about us spreading the "Good News" of Jesus Christ? With a lot people facing difficult times, I am sure they would not mind hearing some good news about how Jesus kept us and brought us through. We are living examples for Jesus Christ and our testimony might just help someone. Everyone has a story to share, because it is through the grace of God that we are here.

God does things for us and through us and it is not we ourselves that has done anything to boast about. Amen! Praise God! Rejoice in the Lord Always!

DAY 84

"Jesus said to him, "If you can believe, all things are possible to him who believes." Immediately the father of the child cried out and said with tears, "Lord, I believe; help my unbelief!"

Mark 9:23-24 NKJV

Father, God in the name of Jesus Christ we come before you asking you, dear Lord, to help our unbelief. Teach us how to grow our faith, humble ourselves and not take you for granted. When we pray dear God, let us learn how to accept your answer, "Be still and wait on you." We are limited in what we can do, our ability, strength and endurance comes from you.

Let us know in our hearts that "What's impossible with men is possible with God." Only You God can make a way out of no way. Lord we want to hold onto your unchanging hands and believe. In Jesus Name, We Pray. Amen! Praise God! Rejoice in the Lord Always!

DAY 85

"Fear not, for I have redeemed you; I have called you by your name; you are Mine. When you pass through the waters, I will be with you; and through the rivers, they shall not overflow you. When you walk through the fire, you shall not be burned, nor shall the flame scorch you. For I am the Lord your God, the Holy One of Israel, you Savior."
Isaiah 43:1-3 NKJV

Lord please give us the knowledge to know that you are always with us, and that the righteous will never be forsaken, and you will always dispatch your angels concerning us. Even though we may feel the world is crushing us, we are not defeated.

Lord, just when we think we are powerless, let us remember you hold all power in your hand, and there is nothing too hard for you. You can do everything, but fail. Lord, teach us to hold on to the faith we profess. We love You Lord. Amen! Praise God! Rejoice in the Lord Always!

DAY 86

"The words of a talebearer are as wounds, and they go down into the innermost parts of the belly."

Proverbs 26:22 KJV

When "tale bearing" or gossip is added to any situation, the damage often cannot be undone. The best way to avoid such a problem is to stop gossip at its beginning. If we hear something that hints of tale bearing, we can ask the speaker not to continue.

And we must resist the temptation to pass along what we hear--even under the guise of a "prayer request." Avoid taking part in any conversation that hints of gossip. Amen! Praise God! Rejoice in the Lord Always!

DAY 87

"Then as He entered a certain village, there met Him ten men who were lepers, who stood afar off. And they lifted their voices and said, "Jesus, Master, have mercy on us!" And one of them, when saw that he was healed, returned, and with a loud voice glorified God, and fell down on his face at His feet, giving Him thanks. And he was a Samaritan. So Jesus answered and said, "Were there not ten cleansed? But where are the nine?"
Luke 17:12-17 NKJV

Let us have an "Attitude of Gratitude." The lepers were in a desperate situation and they called out to the Lord and he healed them. Only one came back to thank God. How many times does the Lord bless us and we don't thank Him?

The Lord has blessed us with miracles, healings, favor, wonderful deeds, deliverance, and eternal life. God blesses us all day everyday. Let us "Thank Jesus for blessing us." Amen! Hallelujah! Rejoice in the Lord Always!

DAY 88

"Rejoice always, pray without ceasing, in everything give thanks; for this is the will of God in Christ Jesus for you."
1 Thessalonians 5:16 NKJV

We should not allow our circumstances to have the power over us and dictate how we will act during a crisis. Let us rejoice always even in the midst of difficult times, because God is in control. And He can turn around all bad things in our life so they work together for our good. Let us pray without ceasing because our prayer tells God that we have faith in Him and that we trust Him. Prayer also helps to keep God in our presence and it reassures us that we are not alone.

So let us pray even when we don't feel like it. We don't have to thank God for everything that happens to us, but let us be thankful in everything. Evil things are not of God, but we can thank God for His presence and the good He will do. And let us know in every storm we go through, God has a lesson; a blessing waiting for us. No matter how we feel about our circumstances, let us Praise the Lord anyhow! Amen! Praise God! Rejoice in the Lord Always!

DAY 89

"You therefore must endure hardship as a good soldier of Jesus Christ."
                    2 Timothy 2:3 NKJV

Hardships, trials and tribulations are going to come our way and we can't fall apart or crawl under a rock. Soldiers or athletes must endure vigorous training in order to win and obtain the victory. Weight trainers must sacrifice to obtain the results they want. We can win and obtain the victory over our circumstances if we sacrifice, are patient and wait on the Lord.

Let us keep on fighting our way through despite our situation, call on the Lord for strength, and realize winning is more rewarding. Yes, we can win. Let us receive and utilize the power in Christ, which he gives us through His grace to endure and win. God will give us the victory and we will give Him the glory. Amen! Praise God! Rejoice in the Lord Always!

DAY 90

"But no man can tame the tongue. It is an unruly evil, full of deadly poison. With it we bless our God and Father, and with it we curse men, who have been made in the similitude of God. Out of the same mouth proceed blessing and cursing. My brethren, these things ought not to be so."

James 3:8-10 NKJV

Cursing out someone or cursing to make a point does not make us a better person; actually, it shows our weaker side. The use of foul language is not of God. The unruly tongue can cause great hurt, pain and divisiveness. We can tame the tongue with the strength from the Holy Spirit.

Let us pray to God daily and ask Him to order our words in this evil world. The tongue is very light in weight, but the heaviest to control. Let us be of God and use our tongue for praising, worshiping, and uplifting. Amen! Praise God! Rejoice in the Lord Always!

DAY 91

"I know that nothing is better for them than to rejoice, and to do good in their lives, and also that every man should eat and drink and enjoy the good of all his labor—it is the gift of God."

Ecclesiastes 3:12 NKJV

Don't worry, be happy. God wants us to celebrate and enjoy life, do good and be happy. God does not want us to worry. God is our key to true happiness. Only He can unlock the door and show us the way. We can't find happiness or be totally satisfied with earthly pleasure, pursuit and the material stuff we accumulate.

True happiness and satisfaction with our life comes only when we follow God's guidelines for living, take each day as a gift from God, thank Him for it, and serve Him in it. Let us follow God to the road of true happiness. Amen! Praise God! Rejoice in the Lord Always!

DAY 92

"To everything there is a season, A time for every purpose under heaven: A time to be born, And a time to die; A time to plant, And a time to pluck what is planted; A time to kill, And a time to heal; A time to break down, And a time to build up; A time to weep, And a time to laugh; A time to mourn, And a time to dance."

Ecclesiastes 3:1-4 NKJV

We go through cycles of life and God has a plan for us all. God has a reason and a season for everything, we might not understand why. However, let us trust God. He is the Master and He has a master plan. God's time is not our time and nothing happens by chance. We can find joy and peace with God and within ourselves if we accept God's timing. Amen! Praise God! Rejoice in the Lord Always!

DAY 93

"Noah was a just man, perfect in his generations. Noah walked with God. The earth also was corrupt before God, and the earth was filled with violence."

Genesis 6:9b,11 NKJV

80

Like Noah, we too are surrounded by a world that is corrupt and filled with violence. However, Noah did not follow the sins of the world. Noah overcame the sins of the world with God's help. Noah was not perfect, but he lived a life of faith and obedience to God. Noah loved God more than the sins of the world. We too can overcome the sins of the world, triumph over evilness and please God.

With prayer and the help of the Holy Spirit, we can walk a life of faith and obedience. Let us command our destiny a life of obedience to God or to the sins of the world. Amen! Praise God! Rejoice in the Lord Always!

DAY 94

"Be not far from me, for trouble is near; for there is none to help."
                    Psalm 22:11 NKJV

We can always count on the Lord to be near when we need Him. God will never let us to walk the rough roads alone. We just need to call on the Lord for He is just a prayer away. Call on Him! God wants to be the one we call and depend on, not our family or friends.

God is faithful. He will come to our rescue. God loves us and He keeps us in His presence. Let us keep God in our presence so when trouble comes, we know whom to call. Meditate on His word day and night.

If we call on the Lord, He will stand beside us through every challenge we face. God will then give us the victory over our troubles and we will give Him the glory. Amen! Praise God! Rejoice in the Lord Always!

DAY 95

"For he does not know what will happen; so who can tell him when it will occur?"
Ecclesiastes 8:7 NKJV

We serve an all-knowing God. Nothing happens by chance or by coincidence. Everything happens according to God's will and purpose. God has control of everything under the sun. We might not understand some of the things that happen to us, but God has a reason and a season for everything. We can't say when this or that will happen, because we don't know only God knows for sure. God works things out in His time not ours and He is always right on time.

Therefore, let us always trust the Lord and consult Him for everything. Never give up, no matter how long it takes or how bad it might seem. Wait upon God to work everything out, and persevere because that blessing could be at the door. God knows best, trust Him! Amen! Praise God! Rejoice in the Lord Always!

DAY 96

"Praise be to the Lord, to God our Savior, who daily bears our burdens."
Psalm 68:19 NIV

We don't have to carry the weight of the world on our shoulders. Our Father in heaven is willing to carry our burdens for us. Through the grace of God, we can be freed of the burdens that weigh us down with worry, stress and depression. However, in order to be free we must give our burdens to God daily in prayer and leave them with Him. Don't try to pick them back up and think we are helping God.

God does not need our help today, tomorrow or ever. He can do it alone. God says "Come to me, all you who are weary and burdened, and I will give you rest" Matthew 11:28 NIV. Let us come before the Lord daily in prayer. ASAP: Always Say A Prayer! Amen! Rejoice in the Lord Always!

DAY 97

"Thus says the Lord, the God of David your father: "I have heard your prayer, I have seen your tears; surely I will heal you."
2 Kings 20:5 NKJV

God is a healer; He will heal us. God can heal us spiritually and physically. However, sometimes God only chooses to heal us spiritually. There are many benefits to a spiritual healing. With a spiritual healing, we can once again have faith, trust and hope in God. We can then find the strength and endure the pain to overcome any type of affliction.

A spiritual healing from the only true living God will give us joy and peace that transcends all understanding. A strong spirit can produce and support a physical healing. Let us pray and thank God for a spiritual healing. Amen! Praise God! Rejoice in the Lord Always!

DAY 98

"You will show me the path of life; in your presence is fullness of joy; at Your right hand are pleasures forevermore."
Psalm 16:11 NKJV

We can find real everlasting joy in a relationship with Jesus Christ. Jesus Christ is our Bread of Life and He is the path to a richer fuller life filled with joy and peace. Having real joy in Christ goes much deeper then being happy. Happiness does not last forever and it changes with our external circumstances. However, real joy is everlasting and it is based on the presence of God within us. Real joy allows us to find contentment and rejoice in the midst of our troubles.

As we draw closer to God, the deeper the relationship, the more unwavering our joy becomes. We can rejoice and celebrate life once we find real joy in Christ. Let us be joyful! Amen! Praise God! Rejoice in the Lord Always!

DAY 99

"Do not merely listen to the word, and so deceive yourselves. Do what it says."
James 1:22 NIV

God's Word is everlasting and it has the greatest power. Be transformed by the renewing of your mind, through the Word of God. "All Scripture is God-breathed and is useful for teaching, rebuking, correcting and training in righteousness, so that we may be thoroughly equipped for every good work" (2 Timothy 3:16).

Get into God's Word and let the Word get into you! God's Word teaches us how to walk right and talk right so we can be alright. Be a doer if you want to be like Christ. Amen! Praise God! Rejoice in the Lord Always!

DAY 100

"Though the fig tree may not blossom, nor fruit be on the vines; though the labor of the olive may fail, and the fields yield no food; though the flock may be cut off from the fold, and there be no herd in the stalls- yet I will rejoice in the Lord, I will joy in the God of my salvations."

Habakkuk 3:17-18 NKJV

Even though everything seems to be crumpling around us let us continue to have faith and trust in the Lord anyhow. The Lord can turn any situation around and nothing is over until the Lord says it is over. We can't let the events around us control our life, because God is in control and He is with us. In the midst of trouble, rejoice in the Lord anyhow. Trouble doesn't last forever. Amen! Praise God! Rejoice in the Lord Always!

DAY 101

"Delight yourself in the Lord and He will give you the desires of your heart."
Psalm 37:4 NIV

We all have something that we desire and would like to posses. Well, we can have it and more. Our God, our Father, is the richest man in the world. He created everything and everything is His. And He can give us anything that our heart desires, big or small. We might desire something that seems impossible for us to obtain, but let us know it is not impossible for God to obtain it and give it to us (remember He owns everything).

God wants to share all of His creations with us because He loves us, and He wants us to enjoy life. However, God wants some love too, and He wants us to show it. Out of our own free will, He wants us to delight ourselves in Him and in His word. Let us express our love to God by seeking and obeying Him with all of our heart, soul and mind. Let us not only remember God when we desire something. We all want to be loved. Amen! Praise God! Rejoice in the Lord Always!

DAY 102

"If My people who are called by My name will humble themselves, and pray and seek My face, and turn from their wicked ways, then I will hear from heaven, and will forgive their sin and heal their land."
2 Chronicles 7:14 NKJV

God does not approve of everything we do and He wants us to be willing to change because of some of those things, we are blocking our blessings. So brothers/sisters, let us know we have some repairs to make on the inside. Let us be transformed by the renewing of our mind. God knows we will never be perfect, but He wants us to strive toward putting our best foot forward. We can do it if we keep our mind on the Lord. And with prayer, we can learn how to walk right, talk right, and do right so we can be alright.

God sees greatness in all of us, and He does not want anything we do to hinder us from achieving that greatness and living the wonderful life He has laid out for us. God wants us to enjoy the "Good life." Let us not be our own worst enemy and throw away our blessings because we refuse to change. Change can be good! Amen! Praise God! Rejoice in the Lord Always!

DAY 103

"*My son, if sinners entice you, do not consent.*"
Proverbs 1:10 NKJV

Many people believe if we are not living a life filled with lust, drunkenness, and love of material things, then we really are not living and enjoying life. However, that is so far from the truth. Living a life pleasing to God is more rewarding and enjoyable.

God gives life to our body, soul and spirit when we begin to walk in His ways. And, we begin to accomplish and obtain more than we ever expected. Sin is attractive, enticing and can be fun, but let us remember the fun is short-lived and it leads us to nowhere good.

So let us not grow weary in doing good because in due time, it leads to more blessings, more prayers reaching God, more opportunities, more success, and more prosperity. "Blessed is the man who walks not in the counsel of the ungodly" (Psalm 1:1). Let us make better decisions so we can live a better life. Amen! Praise God! Rejoice in the Lord Always!

DAY 104

"But seek first the kingdom of God and His righteousness, and all these things shall be added to you."

Matthew 6:33 NKJV

We usually put many things before God. We allow people, objects and goals to bump God out of His first place. When it comes to God, we are always too busy, tired or don't have enough time. God calls us to put Him first, before everybody and everything.

He wants to be the center of our life. He wants to be the one that we depend on for all things. Let us know as we draw closer to God, He draws closer to us and life gets better. We find ourselves with more strength, more hope, more faith, more joy and more peace because God lifts all of our burdens and manages all of our affairs. God finds favor in people who put Him first and He adds on to them blessings.

We have to decide what is more important in our life, things of God or the limited things that we can do and give ourselves. We can't beat God's giving. Amen! Praise God! Rejoice in the Lord Always!

DAY 105

"Watch and pray so that you will not fall into temptation. The spirit is willing, but the body is weak."

Matthew 26:41 NIV

Satan is smart and cunning...he tempts us with things that are against God and pleasing to the flesh. The serpent tempted Adam and Eve to disobey God and eat from the tree of the knowledge of good and evil. However, we can overcome temptation by watching (being aware of the possibilities of temptation) and praying. Satan will tempt us where and when we are most vulnerable.

Sometimes in our own frail human strength, it is difficult to resist temptation. However, if we call on God through prayer for spiritual strength, we can gain the victory over Satan. Tell Satan, "Get thee behind me!" Amen! Praise God! Rejoice in the Lord Always!

DAY 106

"You will keep him in perfect peace, whose mind is stayed on You, because he trust in You."

Isaiah 26:3 NKJV

Trouble is all around us and we can't avoid it. We have troubles at home, work, with our family, with our relationships. No matter where we turn, trouble is there taking away our peace of mind. Well, brothers/sisters, let us know we are too blessed to be stressed. We are children of the Most High God and we don't have to be stressed or shaken by chaos when it comes our way. God is here for us and He wants to exchange all our problems for peace that only He can give.

However, let us know we can only find the peace that God gives by focusing and meditating on Him and His word daily. If our heart is devoted to God, we can find perfect peace in the midst of the wildest storm. The peace that God gives us, the world can't give to us. So don't let the world take it away. We are too blessed to be stressed! Let Go, Let God! Amen! Praise God! Rejoice in the Lord Always!

DAY 107

"And God sent me before you to preserve posterity for you in the earth, and to save your lives by a great deliverance. So now it was not you who sent me here, but God."
Genesis 45:7-8 NKJV

In Genesis, Joseph revealed to his brothers that it was God who brought him to Egypt for a specific purpose and it was not because of them or their evil schemes. God has a specific purpose for all of us to fulfill. And His "will" will be ultimately done not because of others or their evil schemes made it happen, but because God made it happen.

God may use others to help us arrive at our destination, but it is God who alone has the power to make everything possible. So let us not have fear, but only faith in God because He knows where we are and what is happening to us at all times. And He will work out all evil schemes plotted against us so they work out for His purpose.

We might not understand it at the time or fully see God's purpose, but let us know God has a reason and a purpose for everything and He has not left us alone. When we are afraid or not sure about what is happening, let us know God has His hand on us and nothing evil shall prosper against us. Amen! Praise God! Rejoice in the Lord Always!

DAY 108

"Hear, O Israel, and be careful to obey so that it may go well with you and that you may increase greatly in a land flowing with milk and honey, just as the Lord, the God of your fathers, promised you."

Deuteronomy 6:3 NIV

Let us not miss our chance to live the "Good Life." God is offering us a life full of faith, triumph and serenity. In return, God is just asking us to be obedient to His will and His ways. Being obedient to the Lord does not mean we have a long list of things we can and cannot do (if we do, then we become judgmental) and it does not mean we think we are holier.

It just means we realize that we need Christ's guidance and strength. We can still have a good time and be obedient to the Lord. Amen! Praise God! Rejoice in the Lord Always!

DAY 109

"For whoever calls on the name of the Lord shall be saved."

Romans 10:13 NKJV

Accepting God's invitation of salvation is not a complicated process. We don't have to change, dress up or have a degree; God will meet us right where we are. It just takes us to confess with our mouth and believe in our heart that God has raised the Lord Jesus Christ from the dead. We will then be saved.

Once we open the door and allow God to come into our heart, He will never fail to provide His righteousness, love, grace and mercy. Let us open our heart! There is nobody greater. Amen! Praise God! Rejoice in the Lord Always!

DAY 110

"Praise the Lord! Praise God in His sanctuary; Praise Him in His mighty firmament! Praise Him for His mighty acts; Praise Him according to His excellent greatness! Let everything that has breath praise the Lord. Praise the Lord!"
Psalm 150 1-2, 8 NKJV

When praises go up, blessings come down! Praise the Lord! Hallelujah is the highest praise! All glory and honor belong to the Lord He is worthy to be praised. The Lord loves it when we show Him gratitude for all the many blessings He has bestowed upon us.

Let us praise the Lord even when the sun does not shine. Trust and know that the Lord is working everything out according to His will and purpose. Amen! Praise God! Rejoice in the Lord Always!

DAY III

"In everything do to others as you would have them do to you; for this is the law and the prophets."

Matthew 7:12 TNRSV

This is a Golden Rule by which we should all try to live. Following this Golden Rule will help us to live a much happier and rewarding life. This is because others will treat us the way we treat them. If we treat others with hate and disrespect, that is the only kind of people we will attract to ourselves and they would treat us the same way.

So, if we don't want something done to us, we should not do it to others. Keeping our minds on things that are of God would help us to treat others with respect and kindness. Let us keep showing love and kindness to others even when they don't show it to us, knowing someone else will come along and do the same to them. Amen! Praise God! Rejoice in the Lord Always!

DAY 112

"May the favor of the Lord our God rest upon us; establish the work of our hands for us--- yes, establish the work of our hands."

Psalm 90:17 NIV

Many times, we try to do so many tasks at one time that we end up working hard, going the wrong way, and accomplishing nothing. However, if we call on the Lord daily He will guide us and give us strength to complete the tasks that lay before us. The Lord knows what direction we should go even when we don't. The Lord created us and He knows everything about us. He wrote our life story.

So why not pray to the Lord and ask Him to guide our steps everyday. The more guidance we get from the Lord the less time we spend going the wrong way and working hard. We can't do it alone. There are too many obstacles in the world that could derail our plans. We might not know the direction we are going, but we know the Lord is guiding us. Let us allow the Lord to lead us. Amen! Praise God! Rejoice in the Lord Always!

DAY 113

"I have calmed and quieted my soul."
Psalm 131:2 NKJV

The kind of noise that endangers our spiritual well-being is not the noise we can't escape from, but the noise we invite into our lives. Some of us use noise as a way of shutting out loneliness, shutting out our own thoughts, and as a way of shutting out the voice of God, preventing us from hearing what God has to say. Even if we can't find a place that is perfectly quiet, we need to find a place to quiet our souls, a place where God has our full attention.

Try repeating this scripture until your soul is calm and quiet. Don't let the noise of the world keep you from hearing the voice of the Lord. Amen! Praise God! Rejoice in the Lord Always!

Written by Delorise Reuben-McDuffie

DAY 114

"But one thing I do: Forgetting what is behind (not losing all memory from the past, but leaving it behind as done and settled) and straining toward what is ahead, I press on toward the goal to win the prize for which God has called me heavenward in Christ Jesus."

Philippians 3:13-14 NIV

Let us learn from the past and move on into the present, leaving the past where it belongs -- behind us. Let us press on into the future where God has many blessings waiting for us. God has forgotten about our past, He remembers it no more. He holds nothing we did in our past against us today or in the future. So now it is time for us to release and let go of anything that is hindering us from moving into the future. Whatever it is that is hindering us, let us seek the Lord for guidance for there is no problem He can't solve.

When we hold onto the past, it is difficult for us to move into the future. And, when others try to hold the past against us let us tell them "God has forgiven me and I have moved on into the future." When we put our life in God's hands, He helps us to leave the past behind and grow in the knowledge of Him.. Let us not dwell on the past, but realize we have a more meaningful life ahead of us with Christ Jesus. Amen! Praise God! Rejoice in the Lord Always.

DAY 115

"You yourselves have seen everything the Lord your God has done to all these nations for your sake; it was the Lord your God who fought for you."

Joshua 23:3 NIV

The next time we are feeling hopeless, let us remind ourselves what the Lord has already done for us. And let us know He will do the same again and again. Let us remember the many battles the Lord has already fought for us and won. The Lord has been right there by our side all of the time fighting for us even when we did not notice Him.

He was right there, fought for us and won when our health, finances, marriage, family, and enemies rose up against us. When we had to win the battle over drugs, over alcohol, over smoking and over eating, He was there, too. There is no battle that we have to fight alone. For the battle is the Lord's to fight, not ours.

So let us keep hope alive because the Lord is alive and well, sitting on His throne. The Lord will never leave us alone. Amen! Thank and praise God for all he has done, is doing, and will do for us! Rejoice in the Lord Always!

DAY 116

"Indeed we count them blessed who endure. You have heard of the perseverance of Job and seen the end intended by the Lord – that the Lord is very compassionate and merciful."
James 5:11 NKJV

Life is not a rosy perfect picture. We will endure many hardships, persecutions, trials and tribulations. However, if we hold onto our Lord Jesus Christ and never let go, we can have faith, hope, joy and peace in the midst of our troubles. For it is only the Lord that can sustain us as we weather the storms of life. If we keep our faith and trust in the Lord, we can begin to see the light at the end of the tunnel because the Lord promises to deliver us from all of our troubles.

There is no problem too hard for God to solve. He already has our problem solved even before we know we have a problem.

Each storm has a lesson in it to help us grow in faith and trust in the Lord. Let us pray to the Lord to reveal the lesson we are to learn. And let us keep forging ahead, not allowing the storm to stop us, because God is in control. Amen! Praise God! Rejoice in the Lord Always!

DAY 117

"For the Lord is good and His love endures forever; His faithfulness continues through all generations."

Psalm 100:5 NIV

"God is good all the time, and all the time God is good." God is good to us all of the time. He is our creator, redeemer, deliverer, provider, protector, and healer ... He is our everything!

We can't depend on nobody else like we depend on God because He is always the same and He will never change. If He did something once we can depend on Him to do it again. God is always available. We can call on Him day and night through the good and bad times. God will make a way when there is no way. God will make everything work out for our good. God is always on time, never late.

God keeps all His promises and never lies. We serve an awesome God who will never leave us nor forsake us. Let us look over our life and see the goodness of God. Hallelujah! Thank you God! Amen! Praise God! Rejoice in the Lord Always!

DAY 118

"A soft answer turns away wrath, but a harsh word stirs up anger."
Proverbs 15:1 NKJV

Remove anger and lift your spirits. Next time you feel anger arising, repeat this verse several times and note the effect. You will be amazed at the self-control it gives. When we react to negative remarks or actions, we often say or do something that we can't take back.

Try a different response. Silence will give you time to collect your thoughts and actions, avoiding negative outcomes. Amen! Praise God! Rejoice in God Always!

Written by Delorise Reuben-McDuffie

DAY 119

"But as it is written: "Eye has not seen, nor ear heard, nor have entered into the heart of man the things which God has prepared for those who love Him."

1 Corinthians 2:9 NKJV

We cannot begin to fathom all the blessings the Lord has in store for us, in this life, and for eternity. The Lord has so many new things that He wants to show us, give us and tell us about. There are many new things that we have never heard, thought about, or seen before. For it is the Lord who has all the answers to all of our questions, even to questions we never thought about asking. He holds the only key to our future.

Let us love the Lord and follow in His ways so that we can begin to learn about all the new things He has planned for us. We might not understand all of God's plans, but let us press on anyhow knowing everything is going to work out, because it is God's plan. Let us have hope and faith in the Lord knowing that a wonderful life and eternal future awaits us. The best made plans are the Lord's plans. Amen! Praise God! Rejoice in the Lord Always!

DAY 120

"If anyone serves, he should do it with the strength God provides, so that in all things God may be praised through Jesus Christ."
                    1 Peter 4:11b NIV

We are servants for the Lord...with an important job to do for Christ while we live here on earth. Nobody's job is more important than the others. We are to perform our job to the best of our ability without looking for any reward or praises from man, so that God may receive all the glory. God will reward us for being faithful servants while we are here on earth or when we get to heaven.

If we grow weary working for the Lord, let us use the strength that He will provide. Rebuke selfishness and pride and act out of the spiritual man and not the natural man. Amen! Praise God! Rejoice in the Lord Always!

DAY 121

"But let him ask in faith, with no doubting, for he who doubts is like a wave of the sea driven and tossed by the wind. For let not that man suppose that he will receive anything from the Lord; he is a double-minded man, unstable in all his ways."
                    James 1:6-8 NKJV

We have to believe in order to receive. If we are not going to believe that God will give us what we ask for, then let us not ask. When we ask God for something, we have to have faith that He heard our prayer and that He will answer it. When we doubt God, it tells Him that we are not sure of Him or His abilities.

To have faith in God we must learn how to rely on Him more than ourselves. Amen! Praise God! Rejoice in the Lord Always!

DAY 122

"Therefore we wanted to come to you--even I, Paul, time and again--but Satan hindered us."

1 Thessalonians 2:18 NKJV

Sometimes Satan is going to put obstacles in our way that will hinder our plans because he wants us not to succeed at having hope, faith, peace, or joy. He wants us to to be miserable and hopeless. However, we never have to give up or feel hopeless, we can overcome all of the obstacles that Satan puts in our way. We serve an awesome God that has already overcome the world and all of Satan's obstacles. And He will provide the strength, wisdom and knowledge that we need so that we may go around, go over, go underneath, or go through the obstacles Satan puts in our way.

If God is for us, then nothing Satan puts in our way will stop us; only hinder us for a little while. Let us tell Satan there is no stopping us because our God is the greatest and He is on our side. Don't ever feel hopeless; wait on God, He will always give us the victory. Amen! Praise God! Rejoice in the Lord Always!

DAY 123

"Because the Lord disciplines those he loves, and he punishes everyone He accepts as a son."

Hebrews 12:6 NIV

When we were young and foolish, our parents disciplined us out of love. However, we did not see it that way; we thought our parents were being mean. Now as adults, we thank them because their discipline kept us on the right path. Well, the same goes for God. We are His children and He loves us. God wants to see us walk down the right path and have a great life.

Therefore when we stray, God disciplines us to correct our faults. Remember God disciplines those He loves. Let us not turn away from God during punishment, but ask

Him what lesson we are to learn. Amen!
Praise God! Rejoice in the Lord Always!

DAY 124

*"Jesus Christ is the same yesterday, today,
and forever."*
Hebrews 13:8 NKJV

We can boldly say with faith that "The
Lord is my strength and He will provide." We
can say this because Jesus is immutable
which means He will never change. And we
know that Jesus has already given strength
and provided for Moses, Noah and many
others. So, let us have faith and know He will
also do it for others and us. When Jesus does
something for one person, we can count on
Him to do the same for others and us. He
does not play favorites and He will never
change. If Jesus did something yesterday, we
can depend on Him to do the same today and
forever.

We can have faith and believe in Jesus in
everything He says and does. We are not
serving a "new" Jesus, but the same Jesus
revealed in the Bible. We can read about what
Jesus did in the Bible yesterday for others to
know what He will do today and forever for
us. Take and hold on to Jesus' unchanging

hands. We can depend on the Lord now and forever and that will never change. Amen! Praise God! Rejoice in the Lord Always!

DAY 125

"And the Lord God formed man of the dust of the ground, and breathed into his nostrils the breath of life; and man became of living being. Then the rib which the Lord God had taken from man he made into a woman, and He brought her to the man."
                              Genesis 2:7,22 NKJV

Let us cherish and value the life of others and our own. Life is very precious; let us not waste life by spreading hatred, gossip, envy and jealously. It offers no goodness or adds no benefits to our life. It only takes away and adds misery. God brought us into this world to imitate Him by spreading love, kindness, gentleness, patience, and joy; not hate. Let us rejoice and celebrate the life God has given us despite all the turmoil that is surrounding us because He is in control of everything and we know everything will work out.

The life in which we live is a gift and a blessing from God. We are all created equally, wonderfully and fearlessly in the image of God. Man's body was lifeless until God breathed His "Breath of Life" into our soul. And, God created woman from the rib of man. We are all brothers and sisters in Christ because we came from the same Father. Let us love others and ourselves as our Father loves us. Amen! Praise God! Rejoice in the Lord Always!

DAY 126

"But let patience have its perfect work, that you may be perfect and complete, lacking nothing."

James 1:4 NKJV

God wants to do great things through us and give us the best life has to offer so that we may have the best and lack nothing. However, we can't receive it if we are not willing to be patient. Being patient is an action. It requires us to be still and allow the Lord to lead us. When we have done all we can, let us be patient and wait on the Lord, so He can fill us up with His wisdom and knowledge. We can't do or give ourselves the same thing the Lord gives or does for us. Let us recognize that the Lord has the best to give and that He would never fail us.

When we fail to be patient, we fail at getting the best. Let us pray to the Lord for patience so we won't miss our blessings. Be content and wait the best is coming! Amen! Praise God! Rejoice in the Lord Always!

DAY 127

"Blessed is the man who perseveres under trial, because when he has stood the test, he will receive the crown of life that God has promised to those who love Him."
James 1:12 NKJV

We are going to face many trials in life and we can triumph over them or they can triumph over us. When we face trials of any kind, let us rejoice because the Lord is in control. He is preparing to bless us and take us to a higher level in Him. As we face trials, our faith grows. We learn how to depend on the Lord and we learn how to make Him the center of our life. We learn how to endure and persevere.

This results in the victory over all of our circumstances; a more rewarding and joyful life in Christ Jesus. Let us not act as if life is ending when we face difficult times, but remember it is the beginning of a new and exciting life because God is creating something new in us. Don't let us put a period where God puts a comma. If we don't face

111

trials of any kind, we won't grow. "No pain, no gain." Amen! Praise God! Rejoice in the Lord Always!

DAY 128

"He who dwells in the shelter of the Most High will rest in the shadow of the Almighty. I will say of the Lord, "He is my refuge and my fortress, my God, in whom I trust."
Psalm 91:1-2 NIV

It is good to know that when it is storming in our life, we have God to run to. We don't have to be afraid when the storms come or be scared the Lord will not be around. We can always be sure that the Lord will always be there for us even when no one else is. We can depend and trust the Lord for He is the only one that can sustain us and make everything all right.

During our most difficult times, God will heal our wounds with His love, and give us protection and comfort. The Lord will make us whole again so let us make Him our first refuge and fortress. The Lord watches over us, He knows all about our troubles, and He will never abandon us. Let us put our faith and trust in the Lord. God loves us and He

will never let the righteous be forsaken.
Amen! Praise God! Rejoice in the Lord Always!

DAY 129

*"For the Lord promised David, "By my servant
David I rescue my people from the hand of
the Philistines and from the hand of all their
enemies."*

2 Samuel 3:18 NIV

The Lord will use ordinary people for
extraordinary things. He has equipped each
one of us with Spiritual Gifts to be used for
His Kingdom building. We don't need any
special qualifications, degrees or money. We
need faith; we need to be bold and
courageous so we can step out to find out
what the Lord has for us to do. If we keep
fear instead of faith, we will never realize or
live up to our full potential.

So let us start doing what God has called
us to do without fear, worry or apology. The
Lord will provide us with everything we need.
Therefore when the Lord calls us, let us say
"Lord here I am, use me." Let us come before
the Lord as humble servants ready and willing
to do His will. The Lord used David and He

wants to use us. Amen! Praise God! Rejoice in the Lord Always!

DAY 130

"Praise the Lord! Let them praise the name of the Lord, for He commanded and they were created. Let them praise the name of the Lord, for His name alone is exalted; His glory is above the earth and heaven."

Psalm 148:1,5,13 NKJV

Let all creation lift up the name of the Lord in praise. Let us show God how much we appreciate Him. God does not have to do anything for us, but He does, because He loves us. Let us praise God in the morning, praise Him in the evening, and praise Him all day long. Glory and honor to the King our Father and creator of the heavens and earth.

Thank you Lord for all you have done! We love you for who you are. Let everything that has breath praise the Lord! Amen! Praise God! Rejoice in the Lord Always!

DAY 131

"The Lord watches over you---The Lord is your shade at your right hand; the sun will not harm you by day, nor the moon by night."
Psalm 121:5-6 NIV

God sits high and looks low. God watches over us by day and by night. He never sleeps nor slumbers. God gives us 24 hour/7days of protection. Therefore let our hearts not be troubled, because no matter where we are, the Lord is there. When we go to work, He is there. When we travel to a far away land, He is there. When we go to bed at night, He is there. No matter where, He is there.

So let us throw away that spirit of fear. God keeps His eye on the sparrow, so we know He watches over us too. Amen! Praise God! Rejoice in the Lord Always!

DAY 132

"But do you want to know, O foolish man, that faith without works is dead?"
James 2:20 NKJV

True faith is made complete when we say we have faith and then our good works follow it. We cannot just say we have faith. We must prove it too. Our faith is verified through our actions.

Anybody can just speak words, but our actions show we actually believe what we say. "Actions speak louder than words." Our actions show God our commitment to Him is genuine. We are saved by our faith in Jesus Christ and our changed life is the action that tells God our faith is real. We can't have faith without works. God wants to see some action. Step out on faith; God won't let us fall. Amen! Praise God! Rejoice in the Lord Always!

DAY 133

"Do not be overcome by evil, but overcome evil with good."
                                  Romans 12:21 NKJV

The battle is not ours...it's the Lords. Let us not take matters into our own hands and strike back. God calls us to pray and forgive those that curse, insult, slander or persecute us. Then we are to sit back and allow God to bring the right kind of justice.

When we forgive, we are not excusing their bad behavior. We are just forgiving as God forgives us. If we take revenge, the Lord won't. He knows how to hit them where it really hurts. Let us trust God to fight our battles. He always wins. Amen! Praise God! Rejoice in the Lord Always!

DAY 134

"Three times I pleaded with the Lord to take it away from me. But he said to me, "My grace is sufficient for you, for my power is made perfect in weakness." Therefore I will boast all the more gladly about my weakness, so that Christ's power may rest on me."

2 Corinthians 12:8-9 NIV

None of us like to suffer and feel weak but in our suffering and in our weakness, we can see God's divine power manifested in our life. For when we are weak and suffering, God shows up, empowers us with His spiritual strength, and makes us strong so we can endure and persevere.

During our times of suffering, let us humble ourselves and tell the Lord all about our weakness so His power may rest on us. Let us trust the Lord during our times of troubles because His grace is sufficient! Amen! Praise God! Rejoice in the Lord Always!

DAY 135

"Cast all your anxiety to Him because He cares for you."

1 Peter 5:7 NIV

Why should we carry around our worries when we don't have to? Let us humble ourselves before God and admit we need His help. God wants our worries because only He can handle and solve them all. God is bigger than any problem we might have. Let us trust God fully with our life and give Him our worries in prayer. God is all we need. He cares for us.

So, let us stop worrying about our problems. They interfere with our life, job, thoughts, sleep, health and relationships. Let Go, Let God...God is able! Amen! Praise God! Rejoice in the Lord Always!

DAY 136

"I am greatly encouraged; in all our troubles my joy knows no bounds."

2 Corinthians 7:4b NIV

Sometimes we have to encourage ourselves as we go through the storm. No matter how we feel, let us speak the Word over ourselves. With trouble all around us,

118

remember we can still stand tall. We have to proclaim the victory as we go through the storm.

Let us be encouraged by knowing God is our ever-present help in time of trouble. God is surrounding us and He won't let us fall. God will bring us through just as He did before.

We can be strong through it all. Let us lift ourselves up so trouble won't weigh us down. Be encouraged! Amen! Praise God! Rejoice in the Lord Always!

DAY 137

"Wash me thoroughly from my iniquity, and cleanse me from my sin. Create in me a clean heart, O God, and renew a steadfast spirit within me."

Psalm 51:2,10 NKJV

God will mercifully forgive us for our sins. There is no sin too great to be forgiven. God knows that we will never be sinless, but He wants us to strive to sin less. Sin separates us from the love of God and repentance brings us back.

Therefore, let us repent daily for we sin daily, knowingly and unknowingly. Let us ask God to create within us a pure heart and spirit so we may do His will and not ours. We serve a forgiving God who loves us. Don't let sin separate us from the love of God. Amen! Praise God! Rejoice in the Lord Always!

DAY 138

"Praise the Lord! Blessed is the man who fears the Lord, who delights greatly in His commandments. His descendants will be mighty on earth; the generation of the upright will be blessed. Wealth and riches will be in his house, and his righteousness endures forever."

Psalm 112:1- 3 NKJV

Let us put our trust in the Lord. Many blessings will come to others and us if we fear (respect and revere) the Lord. Nobody else can richly bless us like the Lord. So, why should we be following someone else? We have to choose whom we shall serve.

Let us fear God so all of our other fears will be all gone. Amen! Praise God! Rejoice in the Lord Always!

DAY 139

"He said to them, "The Son of Man is going to be betrayed into the hands of men."
Mark 9:31b NIV

Not only did Judas betray Jesus, we too have betrayed Him. Let us think of the ways we have betrayed Jesus. Then afterwards, let us pray for forgiveness and a change of heart. We betray Jesus in many ways. Some of them are when we choose to do our own will and not His, when we don't trust Him, and when we show a lack of faith. Jesus loves us and He desires to have a good trusting relationship with us.

So let us stop betraying the one person who will never betray us. Let us give Jesus our best and not any less. Amen! Praise God! Rejoice in the Lord Always!

DAY 140

"Then he entered the temple area and began driving out those who were selling. "It is written", he said to them, "My house will be a house of prayer, but you have made it a den of robbers."
Luke 19:45-46 NIV

In the above scripture, Jesus cleared the temple from all of its unrighteousness. Let us follow in Jesus' footsteps and cleanse our temple (body, soul and spirit) of all the things that are not of God. Let us pray to God and ask Him to help us because we can't do it alone. Hate, envy, jealously, lust, drunkenness and selfishness are a few things that we need to cleanse ourselves of.

God created us in His image and not in the image of the world. Let us be more like God and less like the world. Amen! Hallelujah! Rejoice in the Lord Always!

DAY 141

"Many are saying of me, "God will not deliver him."

Psalm 3:2 NIV

We need to be careful of whom we listen to or take advice from. Some people have not recognized the goodness of God in their lives and are blind to the things He does. Yes, "God will deliver us." Let us remember that and store it in our heart.

Not only does the Word of God tell us He will deliver us from our enemies, sorrows, crises, hardships, trials and tribulations. It tells us He will also give us the victory over them. God can deliver us from all things.

So let us trust God and His Word and not allow the spiritual blind to deter us from the things we know to be true about Him. Psalm 118:8 tells us "It is better to trust in the Lord than to put confidence in man. Man can't deliver; God can. Amen! Praise God! Rejoice in the Lord Always!

DAY 142

"Give and it will be given to you. A good measure, pressed down, shaken together and running over, will be poured into your lap."
Luke 6:38 NIV

Let us remember, "It is more blessed to give than to receive." Let us be thankful to God for what we have and share it with others less fortunate. As we give, we will receive much greater. Jesus say, "I tell you the truth, whatever you did for one of the least of these brothers of mine, you did for me" (Matthew 25:40).

Let God use us to be a blessing to others as He is a blessing to us. It is not about how much we give, it's about our giving from the heart. We all have something to give. To name a few things we can give are time, money, food, clothes or just simply, a smile.

Amen! Praise God! Rejoice in the Lord Always!

DAY 143

"Great peace have they who love your law, and nothing can make them stumble."
Psalm 119:165 NIV

God is our peace giver...He will give us peace that the world can't give or take away. If we trust, love and obey the Lord, we can attain perfect peace. Perfect peace will give us the ability to soar above our circumstances.

We will be able to escape the fears, worries and stress that always accompany our problems. We will know without a doubt that the Lord has our back. We then can rejoice in the midst of turmoil.

Let peace accompany our problems and not stress, because we are too blessed to be stressed. Amen! Praise God! Rejoice in the Lord Always!

DAY 144

"The Lord is with me; I will not be afraid. What can man do to me?"
Psalm 118:6 NIV

Let us recognize where our help comes from, then let us put our trust and confidence in him. Our help comes from God, the creator of the heavens and earth so let us put our trust and confidence in Him. God will always be there for us no matter what the circumstances are. When we need the Lord's help, He runs to us and not from us.

We shall never be afraid for God will always protect us and guide us day or night. God is stronger and wiser than any man. His power surpasses all others. No one can do what God has done. Let us trust God! God is our ultimate helper and protector. Amen! Praise God! Rejoice in the Lord Always!

DAY 145

"It is good to praise the Lord and make music to your name O Most High, to proclaim your love in the morning and your faithfulness at night. For you make me glad by your deeds O Lord; I sing for joy at the works of your hands."

Psalm 92:1-2, 4 NIV

"The Lord is good, His love endures forever." Let us bow down before the Lord and thank Him. Thank God for all the blessings, miracles and wonderful deeds He has bestowed upon our loved ones and us. We don't have to wait for any special day to thank God for He is blessing us right now.

Let us show the Lord that we have an attitude of gratitude. We cannot do anything without the Lord so let us thank Him. Amen! Praise God! Rejoice in the Lord Always!

DAY 146

"If you fully obey the Lord your God and carefully follow all His commands I give you today, the Lord your God will set you high above all the nations on earth."
Deuteronomy 28:1 NIV

Like all good parents, God has rules and boundaries set for us to live by. We might not like them, but they are set so that we can have a fruitful and rewarding life. We serve an awesome God that only wants the best for his children. We will be blessed as we strive to walk and talk right. The Holy Spirit is with us to help guide us down the road of righteousness.

God knows we will never be perfect, but He wants us to attempt to get there. Let us keep our eyes on the prize and remember our

Father knows best. Amen! Praise God! Rejoice in the Lord Always!

DAY 147

"Be sober, be vigilant; because your adversary the devil walks about like a roaring lion, seeking whom he may devour. Resist him, steadfast in the faith, knowing that the same suffering are experienced by your brotherhood."

1 Peter 5:8-9 NKJV

The devil chooses his victims, and he does not discriminate. Therefore, let us remain watchful and spiritually fit always. When we become focused on our troubles, we forget to watch for danger and we then become vulnerable to Satan's attacks.

Satan likes to tempt us when we are hungry, angry, lonely and tired. Jesus is our only weapon, so let our mind be stayed on Him. 'Resist the devil and he will flee." Amen! Praise God! Rejoice in the Lord Always!

DAY 148

"But if serving the Lord seems undesirable to you, then choose for yourselves this day whom you will serve. But as for me and my household, we will serve the Lord."
                              Joshua 24:15 NIV

There comes a time in our life when we have to choose whom we will serve. The choice is ours for we have free will. God does not force Himself on us. He wants us come to Him with a willing heart and spirit. We cannot go wrong in serving the Lord.

God has been proven to be loving, awesome, faithful, dependable, forgiving, and kind. God is all we need.   He is our everything. God is at the door knocking; let Him in. Amen! Praise God! Rejoice in the Lord Always!

DAY 149

"I have come that they may have life, and that they may have it more abundantly."
                              John 10:10 NKJV

We all search and want a better life, and God is offering it to us. Out of love and care for us, God gave us His only begotten Son so that we may have life eternally and abundantly. A new car, more money, bigger house or new job will not make our life any better.

Jesus is the only way. He is our key to life. Only Jesus can open doors no other man can open. Jesus gives us a life that is richer, fuller and filled with success and prosperity.

Life with Jesus is better than having silver and gold. Jesus is the Master with the master plan. Let us stop searching and take God up on his offer. Don't delay, follow Jesus today. Amen! Praise God! Rejoice in the Lord Always!

DAY 150

"But those who hope in the lord will renew their strength. They will soar on the wings like eagles, they will run and not grow weary, they will walk and not be faint."

Isaiah 40:31 NIV

With our hope in the Lord, we can overcome many of life's obstacles and accomplish great things. We shall receive our strength from the Lord as we passionately seek and rely on Him instead of ourselves. We will have the ability to soar above the storm like an eagle. Like the eagle, we cannot escape the storm but we can get the strength to rise above it.

REJOICE: A Celebration of Life

We will be able to soar above the storms of illness, finances or loss. Let us remain hopeful and not hopeless. Amen! Praise God! Rejoice in the Lord Always!

DAY 151

"Make every effort to live in peace with all men and to be holy; without holiness no one will see the Lord."
Hebrews 12:14 NIV

God has called us to love one another just as he loves us. God wants us to choose peace over conflict. If someone curses, mistreats or persecute us, we are called to forgive and pray for them. As our relationship with God grows, so shall our relationship with others. We cannot do this with our human strength; but with God, everything is possible.

Let us not be the one who stirs up gossip or conflict, but the one who stirs up peace. When misery comes knocking, close the door. Amen! Praise God! Rejoice in the Lord Always!

DAY 152

"For I know the plans I have for you declares the Lord, plans to prosper you and not harm you, plans to give you hope and a future."
                    Jeremiah 29:11 NIV

Our future has been planned even before we were born and we are predestined for greatness. Our Father is a King, and He has all the power and riches in the world. What God has for us is for us and we should not allow anybody or ourselves deter us from receiving our blessing.

We sometimes block our own blessing by trying to do our own thing. God will take us all the way to the top if we let go and let God. God's plan is always better than our own plan. Trust God! Amen! Praise God! Rejoice in the Lord Always!

DAY 153

"I will strengthen you, Yes, I will help you, I will uphold you with My righteous right hand."
                    Isaiah 41:10b NKJV

When we need strength and help, let us call on the Lord. The Lord is here to strengthen and help us so that we can overcome and have the victory in all that we do. When we can't accomplish our goal with our natural human power, let us know that we can with the Spiritual Power from the Lord.

The Lord will make a way out of no way, open doors no man can open, and send people to help us. Let us stop thinking we can't because we can with the Lord's strength and help.

If we step out of our comfort zone and begin to do what the Lord has called us to do, we will surprise ourselves and see the great things we can accomplish. We serve a great God. Let us trust Him to strengthen and help us. Amen! Praise God! Rejoice in the Lord Always!

DAY 154

"Then you will know the truth, and the truth will set you free."

John 8:32 NIV

It is always good to know the truth. Reading the Bible will lead us to the truth about God and His promises. We should know the truth for ourselves and not always trust what others are saying. There are many false teachers in the world looking to fulfill there own program and not God's. The truth in the Bible will set us free from the bondage of sin and put us on the road to a better life.

If we arm ourselves with the truth, we can fight back and win the war against our trials and tribulations. There is a whole lot of treasure and power in one book. Know the truth! Amen! Praise God! Rejoice in the Lord Always!

DAY 155

"No, in all these things we are more than conquerors through Him who loved us."
Romans 8:37 NIV

On those days when life feels too hard to handle, let us look up and remind ourselves where our help comes from. "We are more than conquerors." With God, we can make it through any storm life throws at us. God's spiritual strength is there for us when our human strength grows weak. So let us walk with pep in our step and joy in our heart knowing that with God we will not be defeated. We are winners and not losers.

Let us remember God never gives us more than we can handle. With God, we can do this! Amen! Praise God! Rejoice in the Lord Always!

DAY 156

"Be still before the Lord and wait patiently for Him; Do not fret when men succeed in their ways, when they carry out their wicked schemes."

Psalm 37:7 NIV

Our eagerness for something can get us into trouble... especially when we see others with what we want. Jealously, lust, greed, and pride are not our friends. They can lead us to want impatiently. Sometimes we let them convince us to do things we would not ordinarily do. When people carry out their wicked schemes to obtain their wants, they usually hurt other people.

Let us pray to God and ask for strength to wait upon Him to supply our needs and give us the desires of our heart. For we know that we serve an on-time God and everything from Him is good and perfect. Amen! Praise God! Rejoice in the Lord Always!

DAY 157

"I know, O Lord, that a man's life is not his own; it is not for man to direct his steps."

Jeremiah 10:23 NIV

We do not have total control over our destiny, but God does. Let us seek God's will for our life and ask Him to order our steps. God will lead and guide us in the direction that we shall go according to His will and purpose. Praying, studying the Bible, and listening to God's small voice will steer us in the right direction.

Trusting in the Lord with our life can mean the difference between success or failure, victory or victim, and better or bitter. We might not know the direction we are going, but we know who is leading us. God knows the way. Amen! Praise God! Rejoice in the Lord Always!

DAY 158

"And surely I am with you always, to the very end of the age."
                                    Matthew 28:20B NIV

If we ever think that we are alone and nobody cares about us or what we are going through, then let us think again. The Lord cares and He is sticking right by our side. God is not going anywhere. The Lord will be with us through the good, bad, happy and sad times. God knows all about our troubles and He is here to help us and supply all of our needs.

The Lord upholds the righteous with His right hand and he does not let us stumble or fall. Let us throw away all fear and rejoice because the Lord is near. Amen! Praise God! Rejoice in the Lord Always!

DAY 159

"For the Lord does not see as man sees; for the man looks at outward appearance, but the Lord looks at the heart."
1 Samuel 16:7b NKJV

Most of us spend too much time beautifying our outward appearance and forget about beautifying the inside. But the true beauty of a person is found on the inside. God looks on the inside and judges us by the content of our heart. God does not consider our outward appearance, or how much money or degrees we have. God looks at our faith and character for they define who we really are.

Let us see others as God sees them for their inner beauty and not their outward appearance. A person's outward appearance can be deceptive to a person's true qualities. Check on the inside! Amen! Praise God! Rejoice in the Lord Always!

DAY 160

"But I have prayed for you, Simon, that your faith may not fail."
                                Luke 22:32 NIV

Don't let our faith fail us now! We need our faith in Christ at all times. Our faith in Christ gives us the ability to triumph over our circumstances. Without faith, all that remains is fear. Fear will block our power and strength from God. Faith saves us from sinking into the pit of depression and despair.

Let our faith be renewed day by day by meditating on the goodness of the Lord and how He brought us thus far. God brought us this far by faith and so let faith take us further. Keep the faith! Amen! Praise God! Rejoice in the Lord Always!

DAY 161

"They took palm branches and went out to meet him, shouting, "Hosanna!" "Blessed is he who comes in the name of the Lord!" "Blessed is the King of Israel!"
                                John 12:13 NIV

A whole multitude of disciples began joyfully rejoicing and praising God in loud voices for the miracles they had seen. Let us too praise God continually for all the many blessings and miracles we have received and seen. God has done so much for us that we can't even count. God is worthy of our praise and thanksgiving. God is the one who redeemed us and who made us brand new.

The impossible happens because God makes it happen. Thank God! Praise God! Amen! Hallelujah! Rejoice in the Lord Always!

DAY 162

"And pray that we may be delivered from wicked and evil men, for not everyone has faith. But the Lord is faithful, and he will strengthen and protect you from the evil one."

2 Thessalonians 3:2-3 NIV

Prayer and the Word of God is our only ammunition against Satan and his schemes. Jesus overcame the world and we too can overcome the world with the strength and protection from the Lord. We no longer have to be friends of the world and a part of their evil schemes. God is faithful and He will deliver us from the evil one.

God has a plan for the wicked and evil men "For the wages of sin is death" (Romans 6:23). For with God, we have eternal life. Let us choose life over death. Amen! Praise God! Rejoice in the Lord Always!

DAY 163

"For where two or three are gathered together in My name, I am there in the midst of them."

Matthew 18:20 NKJV

It is good to gather and fellowship with people of the same mindset. Jesus is in the midst of small groups and He hears our prayers. There is great joy in fellowshipping because we just never know when our presence, concern or testimony will help and give strength to someone.

The Christian journey is not easy and we will encounter many obstacles that will discourage us so we need to be there to uplift and inspire each other to persevere. When we gather together in Jesus' name, He is right there. Amen! Praise God! Rejoice in the Lord Always!

DAY 164

"The Virgin's name was Mary. The angel went to her and said, "Greetings you who are highly favored! The Lord is with you."
Luke 1:27-28 NIV

Mary was obedient to God and He chose her for the most important acts of service. God will choose us too for extraordinary things if we trust Him. We don't have to worry about being qualified, because when God calls us to do something, He will be with us and prepare us for it. God always has a better plan for us. We might want to become a CEO of a company, but God might want us to own that company.

When God finds favor in us, we don't know where it will lead, but it will be good. Amen! Praise God! Rejoice in the Lord Always!

DAY 165

"The Virgin will be with child and will give birth to a son, and they will call him Immanuel—which means, "God with us."
Matthew 1:23 NIV

Most names have meanings and it tells us something about the person. Well, there is a great power in God's name. God's name tells us that we could depend on Him because He is with us. God promises to never leave nor forsake us. Let us remember Psalm 23:4 "Even though I walk through the valley of the shadow of death, I will fear no evil; For You are with me."

If the Lord is with us, then nobody can win against us. Let us know in our heart that God is with us. Amen! Praise God! Rejoice in the Lord Always!

DAY 166

"They replied, "Believe in the Lord Jesus, and you will be saved---you and your household."
Acts 16:31 NIV

John 3:16 tells us that "God so loved the world that He gave His only begotten Son that whoever believes in Him should not perish, but have everlasting life." This is a free gift from God to us and we cannot do anything to earn it.

Let us show God we love Him too by accepting His Son. Jesus was crucified for us so our sins would be forgiven and we could have a chance at a better life.

Let us take hold of what is so freely given to us. Don't pass up the chance to draw close to God. We can't go wrong. Amen! Praise God! Rejoice in the Lord Always!

DAY 167

"Keep on loving each other as brothers, do not forget to entertain strangers, for by so doing some people have entertained angels without knowing it."

Hebrews 13:1-2 NIV

Let us treat all people the same way we would like to be treated. Don't let their race, creed, color, gender or financial status determine how we would treat someone. Let us show love to all people even if we do not agree with what they are doing.

We could love the person, but hate the sin. We all have the same Father and Brother (God and Jesus) and we all are covered with the same blood. We were not sent here to be judge or jury over anybody.

However, if we continue to be an imitator of God and show love to everyone, we won't miss the opportunity to entertain an angel. Amen! Praise God! Rejoice in the Lord Always!

DAY 168

"I lift up my eyes to the hills---where does my help come from? My help comes from the Lord, the maker of Heaven and earth."
                    Psalm 121:1-2 NIV

Let us throw worry and fear out the window. Then, let us keep faith and hope alive. Let us trust in the Lord with all of our heart and know without a doubt that He will deliver us from all of our troubles.

When everything looks hopeless, look to God. He can make a way out of no way. God is able. He is our helper at all times. Whatever we need, God will supply.

Let us not look down, but look up to where our help can be found. Amen! Praise God! Rejoice in the Lord Always!

DAY 169

"Come, let us bow down in worship, let us kneel before the Lord our maker; for He is our God and we are the people of His pasture, the flock under His care."
                    Psalm 95:6-7 NIV

God is our everything. He takes great care of us and He makes sure all our needs are met. Therefore, let us come before God with a submissive attitude and obedient heart worshipping, praising and thanking Him for all the great blessings He has bestowed upon us. We like praises and so does God. He likes it when His children show Him some appreciation.

When praises go up, blessings come down! We serve an awesome God. He molds and holds us, never letting us go. Amen! Praise God! Rejoice in the Lord Always!

DAY 170

"Whenever I am afraid, I will trust in you."
Psalm 56:3 NKJV

We don't have to be afraid anymore. Even when our situation becomes bigger than us, it will never become bigger than God. Fear and worry will come and try to rob our soul of its joy, but we won't let it. We will remember that we don't have anything to fear because God sees every tear and hears every prayer. God knows what we are going through and He is already working it out.

God is our strength. He will guard our heart and mind in times of trouble. God's power can never be defeated so fear not. Trust God and fear not! God cares! Amen! Praise God! Rejoice in the Lord Always!

DAY 171

"In His love and mercy He redeemed them; He lifted them up and carried them all the days of old."

Isaiah 63:9 NIV

God saved us from ourselves. We were our own worst enemies living in darkness according to the world. We were headed for destruction. When God lifted us up out of the slimy pit, dusted us off, and gave us a new heart, He called us His Children. By the grace of God, we are saved. We are new creatures with a new mindset. Our old self is gone. God turned our life around and now we are destined for greatness.

Let us come to God just as we are for only He can turn our life around. Amen! Praise God! Rejoice in the Lord Always!

DAY 172

"For unto us a Child is born, Unto us a Son is given; And the government will be upon His shoulder. And His name will be called Wonderful, Counselor, Mighty God, Everlasting Father, Prince of Peace."
Isaiah 9:6 NKJV

Jesus is the light of the world, our great deliverer and Messiah. Jesus is so wonderful to us in so many different ways and there is nobody else that can compare. He is Jesus all by himself. Jesus is all knowing and all-powerful. He will do us no wrong. We serve a Mighty God who will be our Father for eternity.

Jesus Christ is the light of the world. He seeks peace and justice at all times. Jesus is where we will find faith, hope, trust, joy, and peace. Amen! Praise God! Rejoice in the Lord Always!

DAY 173

"He must increase, but I must decrease."
John 3:30 NKJV

We must be willing to decrease in importance so that the Holy Spirit may increase. In order for God's will to be done in our life, we have to be willing to humble ourselves and move out of the way. God can't do His thing in our life if we are trying to do our own thing. We have to take the focus off ourselves and focus on the Kingdom of God. We have to be willing to put our pride to the side and surrender our body, soul and spirit to God. We can't walk in the spirit if we are not being led by the spirit.

Let us not get in the way of our own success by acting as if we are more important than God. Let us move out so that the Holy Spirit may move in. Amen! Praise God! Rejoice in the Lord Always!

DAY 174

"Whatever is commanded by the God of heaven, let it diligently be done for the house of the God of heaven."
                          Ezra 7:23 NKJV

The Lord is going to call us to perform certain tasks. So we can help spread the Gospel and build His Kingdom here on earth. Whatever task God gives us to do, let us do it to the best of our ability knowing that we are doing it for the glory of God. The task might become hard and seem impossible, but let us not be fearful or quit because whatever task He gives us, He will qualify us to perform it.

So when God calls, let us step out in faith knowing He is going to guide us all the way. Let us trust God and not give up on Him because He will not give up on us. Keep the faith and know that with God, we will succeed in any task He calls us to do. Amen! Praise God! Rejoice in the Lord Always!

DAY 175

"Now a certain man was there who had an infirmity thirty-eight years."

John 5:5 NKJV

Many of us have been physically ill for a long time and have begun to feel like life is over, useless and hopeless. However in spite of our infirmities, let us acknowledge Jesus' powerful greatness and know that with Jesus, there is always hope. Everything happens for a reason and Jesus can use our situation so that it produces some good for others and us. No matter what state we are in physically, we can still live a joyful life and be used by the Lord.

Let us pray to God for a spiritual healing and then allow Him to use us according to His will and purpose. God does not limit us, we limit ourselves. "We can do all things through

Christ who strengthens us." Amen! Praise God! Rejoice in the Lord Always!

DAY 176

"Through the Lord's mercies we are not consumed, because His compassions fail not. They are new every morning; Great is Your faithfulness."
Lamentations 3:22-23 NKJV

It is common for man to sin knowingly and unknowingly everyday. "We all fall short of the Glory of God." However, let us rejoice because we serve an Awesome God who is merciful and promises everyday to forgive all of our sins. God will remember our sins no more and restore us to a right relationship with Him. Our sins create a wedge between God and us, and our repentance closes that wedge.

There is no sin God won't forgive if we approach His throne of grace with a changed heart. Hallelujah! If it had not been for the Lord on our side, we don't know where we would be. Amen! Praise God! Rejoice in the Lord Always!

DAY 177

"Forget the former things; do not dwell on the past. See, I am doing a new thing!"
                              Isaiah 43:18-19A NIV

Let us not get stuck in the past...let us just reference the past for lessons learned. When we fail to leave the past behind, we fail to move in the future. When we accept Jesus Christ as our Lord and Savior, our old self and our old way of thinking are gone.

We are new creatures with a new life. Jesus takes our past and throws it away for it to be remembered by Him no more. Even though God forgets our past, many of us hold on to it. When we carry our past with us, it stops us from being successful and prosperous.

Remember, God has started a new thing in us. Our old life now becomes our testimony, letting others know "With God there is hope and everything can be new again." Amen! Praise God! Rejoice in the Lord Always!

DAY 178

"Thus saith the Lord, which maketh a way in the sea, and path in mighty waters.
Isaiah 43:16 KJV

Nothing is too hard for God...when things seem hopeless, rejoice and know that the Lord can make a way out of no way. When times are hard and there is trial and pain, hold on to what we know God has already done. God can turn our situation around just when we are about to give up. So don't give up.

Our blessing is coming!! The enemy cannot form any weapon against us that can prosper. Let us hold on, wait on the Lord, and He will turn that frown into a smile. Amen! Praise God! Rejoice in the Lord Always!

DAY 179

"Dear friends, let us love one another, for love comes from God."
1 John 4:7 NIV

We all live in this world together so let us learn how to get along and love one another. Let us show more kindness and less selfishness towards one another. Life will be more enjoyable for all of us if we expressed more love.

God is a great example of what true love is and what true love does. He does everything out of love. God loves and forgives us despite some of the things we might say and do because He knows that none of us is perfect. He values our relationship and His love for us is greater than sin.

As God loves us, let us love our brothers/sisters. True love forgives a multitude of sins. Love is a choice and an action, so let's do it. Love gives life to the body, soul and spirit. Make someone's day; smile and show them some love. Amen! Praise God! Rejoice in the Lord Always!

DAY 180

"So Joshua said to the children of Israel, "Come here, and hear the words of the Lord your God."

Joshua 3:9 NKJV

The Lord has a lot to say to us each day, but most of the time we are too busy to take the time to listen. We take time out for gossip, the phone, the TV, our friends, but not the Lord. What the Lord has to say to us is more important than anything else we listen to. If we just stop and listen to what the Lord has to say, we could avoid some of the mistakes we make. How are we going to know what the Lord wants us to do if we don't stop and listen?

Each day before we start our day, let us find a quiet place to pray and listen to what the Lord has to say. Spending time listening to the Lord is time well spent. Amen! Praise God! Rejoice in the Lord Always!

DAY 181

"But those who suffer he delivers in their suffering; he speaks to them in their affliction."

Job 36:15 NIV

In our lifetime, we are going to encounter some hardships that will cause us to worry and cry. However, the Lord wants us to know that we are not alone and that He is here for us. Jesus tells us in John 14:1 "Do not let your hearts be troubled. Trust in God; trust also in me."

So, when we encounter those hardships in life, let us remind ourselves of that scripture. Let us not focus on our situation or worry about how things are going to work out.

Let us just focus on the goodness of God and trust Him to deliver us from our suffering. When we begin to acknowledge God's powerful greatness, we can then begin to trust Him to solve our problems. Let go, let God! Amen! Praise God! Rejoice in the Lord Always!

DAY 182

"You may say to yourself, "My power and the strength of my hands have produced this wealth for me." But remember the Lord your God, for it is he who gives you the ability to produce wealth, and so confirms his covenant, which he swore to your forefathers, as it is today."

Deuteronomy 8:17-18 NIV

When we look around and see all the beautiful things that we own, let us remind ourselves that it was God that made it all possible and not ourselves. Let us know it was God that made our finances right so we can buy that car, home, jewelry, or take that trip. Let us not pat our own ourselves on the back. Instead, let us give God all the glory He deserves through praise and thanksgiving.

God is one who has blessed us with the ability to produce wealth for our family and ourselves. He is the one who blesses us with the strength we need to overcome any obstacles so we can get the job done.

So when the blessings come, let us not push God out of the picture and act like we did everything ourselves. If it had not been for the goodness of God, where would we be? Thank Him, don't forget Him. Let us remember the Lord when we have a little or a lot, for it is better to have the Lord than silver or gold. Amen! Praise God! Rejoice in the Lord Always!

DAY 183

"Thus says the Lord of hosts: "Consider your ways!"

Haggai 1:7 NKJV

Every now and then, it is good for us to look at ourselves and evaluate how we are living. There are always areas in our life that we can improve on. God wants us to concentrate mostly on improving our spiritual life. God wants us to be spiritually fit. God knows a healthy spiritual life is far more rewarding and productive. A healthy spiritual life will improve our life physically, mentally, emotionally and socially.

All the areas of our life will improve. A better quality of life comes with a better spiritual life. Let us strive to become spiritually fit so all areas of our life will be fit. Amen! Praise God! Rejoice in the Lord Always!

DAY 184

"Yet give attention to your servant's prayer and his plea for mercy, O Lord my God. Hear the cry and the prayer that your servant is praying in your presence this day."

1 Kings 8:28 NIV

We all want God to hear our prayers when we pray to Him. However, God will close His ears to prayers from some of us. When our prayers are not being answered, let us not blame God, but blame ourselves because there are things that we are holding on to that will hinder our prayers to God. Things that we hold on to that hinder our prayers are refusing to live according to God's will, unconfessed sin, unforgiving spirit, doubt, and selfish motives.

James 5:16 tells us "The effective, fervent prayer of a righteous man avails much." Prayer is powerful and important so let us remove all static and interference from the main line. Amen! Praise God! Rejoice in the Lord Always!

DAY 185

"Get behind me, Satan!" he said. "You do not have in mind the things of God, but the things of men."

Mark 8:33 NIV

Satan comes to kill and destroy us. There is no good in Satan; he is cunning, a liar, and a murderer. Satan is the total opposite of God and he wants us to follow him, and not God. However Saints, let us know we do not have to follow Satan and accept the negative thoughts he will throw at us.

With God, we can control our mind and what we let in. We can open our mind to things of God and close our mind to the things of Satan. Let us not give Satan any power over our mind. Let us send him away defeated. Therefore, when Satan tells us we can't, we say we can because God says He will strengthen us so that we may do all things.

God has a future full of blessings, prosperity and success planned for us and Satan will attempt anything to destroy those plans. Let us keep our mind set in one direction towards God. God is more powerful and always has the victory over Satan.

So when Satan comes sneaking around, let us repeat what Jesus said, "Get behind me

Satan!" Amen! Praise God! Rejoice in the Lord Always!

DAY 186

"The Lord bless you and keep you; the Lord make His face shine upon you and be gracious to you; the Lord turn his face toward you and give you peace."
                              Numbers 6:24-26 NIV

Lord, we come humbly before you in prayer so that all may be well with us.

Lord be pleased with all that we may do so that your favor may always rest upon us. And when we do stray to the left or to the right, Lord we ask for your forgiveness, mercy and compassion. Protect us Lord as we go about our day to day activities. Keep us away from any harm and danger that may come our way. Lord please order our words and steps in this ever-changing world so that we may have your approval over our life.

God we know with you, we can find peace that transcends all understanding because the peace you give, the world can't give or take away.

Lord, we love you with all of our heart. In Jesus Name, we pray. Amen. May God's divine favor rest upon all of us forevermore. Amen! Praise God! Rejoice in the Lord Always!

DAY 187

"These things I have spoken to you, that in Me you may have peace. In the world you will have tribulation; but be of good cheer, I have overcome the world."

John 16:33 NKJV

Jesus tells us things so that we will lose all fear and find hope in Him. Jesus wants us to know that with Him, we will have peace and in the world, we will have tribulation. In the world, Jesus was faced with tribulation and so will we. Jesus overcame the world and so can we. So despite the troubles that we are inevitably to face, let us not become discouraged and hopeless.

As long as we accept Jesus, we have the victory over all of our tribulations. Jesus has already won the ultimate victory. So in Him, we will find everlasting peace. Jesus tells us in John 14:27 "Peace I leave with you, my peace I give to you; not as the world gives do I give to you." Keep the Peace! Amen! Praise God! Rejoice in the Lord Always!

DAY 188

"Oh, give thanks to the Lord! Call upon His name; make known His deeds among the peoples! Sing to Him, sing psalms to Him; talk of all His wondrous works."
1 Chronicles 16:8-9 NKJV

Shout for joy and give God His glory. Let us lift our eyes and hands up to the Lord and thank Him for what He has done. Let us share the Lord's goodness with others. The Lord is so good to us and we have a lot to be thankful for. Right now, some of us are facing many challenges and don't feel like there is anything for us to be thankful. But, there is still a lot for us to be thankful.

Let us be thankful because the Lord is with us as we confront our challenges and He provides the strength we need to overcome them. The Lord is great and His love endures forever. Thank Him!! Amen! Praise God! Rejoice in the Lord Always!

DAY 189

"Before Me no God was formed, nor will there be one after Me. I, even I, am Lord, and apart from Me there is no savior. No one can deliver out of my hand. When I act, who can reverse it?"

Isaiah 43:10b-11, 13b NIV

We serve the only true and living God. God is "Lord of Lords and King of Kings and there is not, nor will there be, another. God is mighty and powerful and He has the last word in everything. As we go through our day-to-day tasks, let us hold onto God's unchanging hands. Let us trust God to guide us in the right direction and give us the advice we need.

With our faith in God, we can triumph over our circumstances and find the serenity we need to sustain our joy. There is only one God and there is no other. Amen! Praise God! Rejoice in the Lord Always!

TELEPHONE INTERVIEW WITH
DR. MAYA ANGELOU

The celebrated poet, playwright, author, actress, director, producer, educator, historian, and civil rights activist shares her faith journey and how she survived the tragedies in her life.

Renee Lindsay-Thompson: Some people say that you are a woman of unshakable faith in God. I would like to write about your faith journey.

Dr. Maya Angelou: I do not have unshakable faith. I might say [to God] I need your help right now. And so I have faith. I'm blessed with that. But everybody, I think it is normal to question. We wouldn't question if that hadn't been a gift of God.

So, sometimes people wonder when I question, and maybe that means I don't have faith; but I don't believe that. I think that when you question, you get closer to God.

RLT: Because you know that it's God.

MA: That's the answer.

RLT: Tell me, how did you survive the tragedies in your life?

MA: Well, some I know how, and some I don't know. That is to say, I think sometimes, we thank God for things we know are gifts from God. However, we don't think about the gifts we don't even know we have.

You know, we turned left up there at the light instead of turning right, not knowing that if we turned right, we'd run right into that "Mack" truck. You know? So, that's a gift.

So, the times when you could have said something rude to a person because he or she was rude to you, and something helped you to hold your tongue, and you didn't squash the person; and that person turns out to be the one who helped you with your brother or helped you with your sister. You see?

All of those are gifts from God. So I am aware of or try to be aware of the gifts I know I can see, I can taste, I can feel. And, I'm also grateful for the gifts God gives me and I don't know anything about it.

So, knowing that, when I am faced with some difficulties, I just thank God immediately; though I pray. If thanking God is prayer, I must pray a hundred times or more than that a day.

I just open the door and I see some flowers growing, and I thank God because there are places where people can't open their doors. And then, they'll have no flowers to see, and then they don't have the appreciation of seeing flowers. So, whatever happens, I thank God for it. And then, I thank the messenger, the person God allowed to bring it to me.

RLT: Yes, yes! Okay! Now, what do you want to say to men and women who are suffering and feeling hopeless and lack of faith?

MA: Well, to women and men but particularly to women, being one so long, I would just ask them to look at their lives and realize that each time you made it over, that was God being your bridge over troubled water. I mean, you went for a job and you got it. And, you might think you got it because you did go to school, and you did wear that particular dress that day. And you didn't get the job because somebody there knew you. Whatever it is, it is an act of God; it is gift of God.

I think the most important thing I can see in this interview is to think of the spiritual, "Take your burdens to the Lord and leave them there." I think that we forget more often than not. We take our burdens to the Lord on our knees and pray, "Take this from me," and then, we get up and take the burdens right back with us. What you have to do is "leave them there."

So, I would say to women who are in unkind situations, relationships, first, "They deserve better!" And the truth is: the tree, the man, the state, the country—none of those things made that woman. God made that woman. Each one of us is a child of God. I am a child of the Most High Idea. I deserve to be treated better. And the person I'm with, whether he or she knows it or not, is a child of God; and I'm obliged to treat that person as well as I possibly can.

RLT: Yes, you treat people like you want to be treated.

MA: Absolutely, because they're made of God. God made them, whether they know it or not, whether they act like it or not. They can act like the biggest bore, the biggest boor, as well. But I, as a child of God, I'm supposed to know how to treat that person.

RLT: In the book, "How Strong Women Pray," Bonnie St. John wrote about your experience in the group led by Frederick Wilkerson, studying "Lessons in Truth," and you read aloud "God Loves Me."

MA: Yes, yes, and when I finally got it, that was 1954, and this morning, 2010, I got it.

RLT: How did that experience change your life?

MA: Oh, everything from then on, I thought if God loves me, there's nothing good that I can't do. If God loves me, Maya Angelou, I can step out on this world stage. I can dare to love somebody. I can learn to be a great cook. I can learn to be a great writer. That's me? God that made bees and mountains and water and stars; that entity, that something loves me, Maya? I just said, "Yes, thank you."

But when I wrote the inaugural poem for President Clinton, I said, "Yes, thank you." I prayed a lot and worked hard. The United Nations asked me to write a poem for the world, for the 50th anniversary of the founding of the United Nations, I said, "Yes, thank you, thank you." And, I went to pray right away. "Lord, you've given me this. Help me."

RLT: What church do you attend today?

MA: I'm a member of Mount Zion Baptist Church in North Carolina. I'm a member of Metropolitan Baptist Church in Washington, D.C. And I'm a member of Glide Memorial

Church in San Francisco. The three ministers got together and they said, "Maya, please don't join any more churches. We've got you coming on both coasts."

RLT: So, whatever coast you're on, you have a church.

MA: I can go right there. And I'm a member in good standing, I want you to know.

DAY 190

"It is God who arms me with strength and makes my way perfect."
2 Samuel 22:33 NIV

Sometimes we find it difficult to accomplish many tasks due to lack of strength and we give up. However, we don't have to give up. When we get tired and feel like we cannot go on, let us call on the Lord. The Lord will arm us with strength during our difficult times so we can keep on moving. When our human strength can't, God's spiritual strength can.

Let us keep going strong and never give up. Trust God, He will make a way somehow. Amen! Praise God! Rejoice in the Lord Always!

DAY 191

"Trust in Him at all times, O people; pour out your hearts to Him, for God is our refuge."
Psalm 62:8 NIV

God will never let us down, we can trust Him to do what He says. Everything God has promised to the children of Israel has come to pass. Let us pour our hearts to God and tell

Him about all that is troubling us. God hears us and we can always trust Him to be there with us and lead us in the right direction.

When we trust God and make Him our refuge, we no longer have to be held captive by our situation. Therefore, no matter what situation we face, let us lean on His everlasting arms. Man is limited in what he can do, but God is unlimited. Let us trust God and make Him our refuge. Amen! Praise God! Rejoice in the Lord Always!

DAY 192

"Turn from evil and do good; seek peace and pursue it."
                                        Psalm 34:14 NIV

If we want peace in the world, let it begin with us. Let us pursue and embrace peace, justice, love and unity not only for ourselves, but also for all humankind. Racism, hatred and evilness are not of God. God is love and peace. So let us imitate God and allow Him to use us as vessels of peace.

God has equipped us with the tools we need to promote and conquer peace. The tools are kindness, gentleness, patience, love, self-control and joy. We have these tools lying within our soul so let us use them. When we see other people being argumentative and spewing hatred let us not join, in let us pray and walk away.

Evil does not benefit anyone for in the end there is always a price to pay. But blessed is the person that shuns evil and seeks peace. For life is better with a frown upside down. Be Happy! Seek Peace! Amen! Praise God! Rejoice in the Lord Always!

DAY 193

"Now as Jesus passed by, He saw a man who was blind from birth. And His disciples asked Him, saying "Rabbi, who sinned, this man or his parents, that he was born blind?" Jesus answered, "Neither this man nor his parents sinned, but that the works of God should be revealed in him."

John 9:1-3 NKJV

Sometimes bad things will happen to us and we did nothing wrong. However, God wants us to know that during those times He is using us to fulfill His purpose. God will use our suffering so others and our faith can grow and He can be glorified. We can only learn to trust God when we are in a challenging situation.

God wants us to know that it is He and not us delivering us out of our troubles. When we suffer for any reason, there is always a lesson to be learned. Let us pray to God for that lesson. Amen! Praise God! Rejoice in the Lord Always!

DAY 194

"Therefore, my dear brothers, stand firm. Let nothing move you. Always give yourselves fully to the work of the Lord, because you know that your labor in the Lord is not in vain."

1 Corinthians 15:58 NIV

Many times when we don't see the good our work is doing, we get discouraged and give up. Well when we do work for the Lord we might not always see the good our work is doing, because the Lord operates in His time and it's for His glory. However, we can be sure someone will be blessed from our labor.

So let us not give up when we don't see any results. We plant the seed, water it, and then the Lord makes it grow. In every opportunity we get, let us do work for the Lord no matter what it is, big or small. We never know whose life we might save. The work we do for the Lord will last forever. "The harvest is plentiful but the workers are few,"

Matthew 9:37. Amen! Praise God! Rejoice in the Lord Always!

DAY 195

"Lord, you establish for us; all that we have accomplished you have done for us."
                    Isaiah 26:12 NIV

Let us not boast about what we have done, but let us boast about what the Lord has done for us. Thanks be to God for allowing us to accomplish many great things. The hand of the Lord is upon us and He guides us down the road of success and prosperity. He bestows us with many blessings.

Let us rejoice and remember, "We can do all things through Christ who strengthens us." The Lord is our strength and we can trust Him to lead us to greatness. Amen! Praise God! Rejoice in the Lord Always!

DAY 196

"Therefore, if anyone is in Christ, he is a new creation; the old has gone, the new has come!"

                    2 Corinthians 5:17 NIV

Let us come to the Lord just as we are. For only God can change us and make us a new creation. God will create in us a new heart and give us a new way of thinking. We can begin life anew and leave our old life behind. God forgives all of our past sins so our past life does not matter anymore. We can walk into the future that God has planned for us with pep in our step and praise in our heart.

Let us thank God for His Amazing Grace. God is Great! Amen! Praise God! Rejoice in the Lord Always!

DAY 197

"They will fight against you but will not overcome you, for I am with you and will rescue you," declares the Lord."
Jeremiah 1:19 NIV

Let us wake up each morning with a smile on our face and joy in our heart, not worrying about the challenges the day will bring. No matter how many and what type of challenges come our way, they won't be strong enough to prosper against us. We don't have to worry because God is on our side. God is our protector and He watches over us day and night.

We serve a Mighty God with great wisdom and He can give us the ability to triumph over any challenge we may face. We might not be able to see the possibility of a victory, but let us have faith and trust in God to be able to give us the victory. God is able. Don't worry, be happy! Amen! Praise God! Rejoice in the Lord Always

DAY 198

"God is just: He will pay back trouble to those who trouble you and give relief to you who are troubled, and us as well."
2 Thessalonians 1:6-7 NIV

As Christians trying to live right, we will be persecuted. Someone is going to become jealous because they see what God is doing in our life. They are going to bring all of their hatred and jealously to our door. They will come trying to destroy and trash your name and character.

But we can rise above their hatred and jealously, and pray for them. We don't have to fight back because we know God fights our battles and He wins every time. God is real and so is karma! Let us leave room for God's wrath. Amen! Praise God! Rejoice in the Lord Always!

DAY 199

"He called out to them, "friends haven't you any fish?" "No," They answered. He said, "Throw your net on the right side of the boat and you will find some." When they did, they were unable to haul the net in because of the large number of fish."

John 21:5-6 NIV

Jesus has many blessings waiting for us and He wants us to redeem them all. Jesus will even instruct us (as He told His disciples in the above scripture) on how to receive them. Our blessings are a gift from God and they will help make our life joyful, peaceful and successful. We should not want to miss out on all that Jesus has for us.

When we don't redeem our blessings, Jesus might give them away to someone else. So, let us stop and not be too busy to listen for Jesus' small voice calling us and telling us how to redeem all that He has for us. Amen! Praise God! Rejoice in the Lord Always!

DAY 200

"I am unworthy of all the kindness and faithfulness you have shown your servant."
Genesis 32:10 NIV

God loves us and He will give us many things that we don't deserve. We can't even earn a lot of what we receive from God. One of the greatest gifts we received and we did not deserve was the "Son of God." God gave us His only begotten Son so that we may have life eternally and abundantly.

Now, isn't that love. God bestowed His grace and mercy upon us, and forgave our sins. God calls us to do as He did. God wants us love and forgive others that may not deserve it. Let us thank God continuously for His love, grace and mercy. Amen! Praise God! Rejoice in the Lord Always!

DAY 201

"How precious to me are your thoughts, O God! How vast is the sum of them ! Were I to count them, they would outnumber the grains of sand. When I awake, I am still with you.
Psalm 139:17-18 NIV

Let us praise the Lord and show Him that we appreciate all that He has done for us and that we have a heart filled with gratitude. We can't count all of the things the Lord has done for they are many. But let us always remember and never forget how good He has been to us.

The Lord has been so good to us and we will never be able to thank Him enough for all that He has done. But let us thank Him anyhow. The Lord showers us with blessings, wonderful deeds, miracles, and healings everyday when we are awake and even as we sleep. The Lord is blessing us right now! Let us thank Him! Hallelujah! Amen! Praise God! Rejoice in the Lord Always!

DAY 202

"If you walk in My statutes and keep My commandments, and perform them, then I will give you rain in its season, the land shall yield its produce, and the trees of the field shall yield their fruit."

Leviticus 26:3-4 NIV

Following in the ways of the Lord is the key to rejoicing and celebrating life. "Jesus is the way and the truth and the life." Jesus' way is the only way for us to have that great everlasting life we all look for. We will be on the right path to many blessings, hope, faith, joy, victory and peace. Many of us have trust issues and don't like following someone else.

We prefer to trust ourselves and do our own thing. We feel we know what we need and what is best for ourselves. Well let us know that the Lord knows more than we do and He knows what we need before we do. Let us walk with the Lord instead of walking alone. He knows the way. Amen! Praise God! Rejoice in the Lord Always!

DAY 203

"But let all who take refuge in you be glad; let them ever sing for joy."
                                        Psalm 5:11a NIV

We can celebrate and have joy, peace and rest in the midst of our trials and tribulations of any kind. Joy, peace and rest are hidden treasures that can be found in all of us. Our worrying suppresses our joy and keeps it hidden. If we take our mind off our problems and continuously keep our mind on the Lord, He will turn our pain into joy, which then leads to peace and rest.

Let us lay our burdens down before the Lord and allow Him to give us a new attitude.

The Lord can handle all of our problems and He doesn't need our help. Let Go, Let God! Amen! Praise God! Rejoice in the Lord Always!

DAY 204

"My flesh and my heart may fail, but God is the strength of my heart and my portion forever."

Psalm 73:26 NIV

Let us recognize that it is the Lord who gives us life. The Lord Mighty and Powerful sustains and preserves our life. The Lord supplies us with strength during life's weakest moments. For when we are weak, then we are strong with power from the Lord. We can make it through anything that life throws our way when we depend on the Lord.

Let us cling to the Lord for there is "nobody greater." The Lord is holding us tight and He promises to never let us go. Let us trust the Lord to be our life support. Amen! Praise God! Rejoice in the Lord Always!

DAY 205

"But be sure to fear the Lord and serve Him faithfully with all your heart: consider what great things He has done for you."
                    1 Samuel 12:24 NIV

Let us slow down, take time out of our busy day, and reflect on all the things the Lord has done for us. The Lord has blessed us so many times in so many different ways and sometimes we are too busy to realize it. It is God who makes our way possible day after day and not things, other people or us. The Lord blessed us and woke us up this morning, not the alarm clock.

Our faith grows and we learn how to depend on the Lord more as we reflect and begin to see His goodness. We were once blind, but now we can see. See the goodness of the Lord all around us!! Amen! Praise God! Rejoice in the Lord Always!

DAY 206

"Then Nathan said to David, "Do all that is in your heart, for God is with you."
1 Chronicles 17:2 NKJV

Many times, we have something in our heart that we would like to do, but we lack faith in God and in ourselves and we don't do it. A lack of faith will cause us to miss out on doing many things we really want to do.

Nothing we want to do is too big for God to handle. God can do all things; nothing is too hard for God. God will make a way even when we don't see a way. Therefore, if we want to do something, let us pray and have faith in God.

God will be with us from start to finish and He will supply all we need in order to succeed. So, if we want to start a business, go to school, buy a house or whatever it may be, let us do it having faith in God first, then ourselves. We can't do it alone, but we can do it with God. Amen! Praise God! Rejoice in the Lord Always!

DAY 207

"You will pray to Him, and He will hear you,"
Job 22:27 NIV

Prayer is powerful. It can change our circumstances and us. Prayer is a personal experience, an intimate connection with God our Father. Jesus prayed to the Father on many different occasions. Faith is essential when we pray.

Through faith, we know that our Father has heard our prayer. Through faith, He will answer our prayer. And with faith, we shall accept His answer. God's answer can be yes, no, or wait. Whatever it is, God's answer is in our best interest.

When we go to God daily in prayer, let us first pray for forgiveness of our sins so there will be nothing blocking our connection to the Father. Amen! Praise God! Rejoice in the Lord Always! ASAP = ALWAYS SAY A PRAYER!

DAY 208

"The sacrifices of God are a broken spirit; a broken and contrite heart O God, you will not despise."

Psalm 51:17 NIV

God is pleased when we come before Him with a humble heart and in a child-like manner, depending on Him for love, care and forgiveness. God wants us to recognize in our heart that we can't do anything without Him.

Let us approach the throne of grace, bow down before the Lord, and worship Him.

Worshiping the Lord comes from an overflow of love and reverence that is ignited by thinking about God and all of His goodness. We serve an awesome God who takes care of us better than we do ourselves. Amen! Praise God! Rejoice in the Lord Always!

DAY 209

"God had planned something better for us so that only together with us would they be made perfect."

Hebrews 11:40 NIV

We have a plan for our life and God has a plan for our life. God's plan is better than our plan. God has great wisdom and knowledge, and His plan calls for us to succeed and not to fail. God will reveal His plan to us when our heart unites with Him.

We can't begin to understand the great things that God has planned for us if we are not united with Him. God's blueprints for our life will teach us how to build a strong foundation that will withstand the test of time and last eternally.

Let us allow God to be the Author of our life story so we can have the number one best seller eternally. Amen! Praise God! Rejoice in the Lord Always!

DAY 210

"And let us not grow weary while doing good, for in due season we shall reap if we do not lose heart."

Galatians 6:9 NKJV

Sometimes we don't feel we are really appreciated for the good we do and we say "Why do it if I am not appreciated." Well, the nice guy might finish last, but he will receive the greatest reward. We might not receive thanks or appreciation from man, but God appreciates the good we do and He will bless us for what we have done. For our reward for doing good comes from the Lord, not man.

Let us know that every time we do something good, God receives the Glory so let us continue to do good to the glory of God. If we don't receive our blessings while on earth for doing good, know for sure we will receive them in heaven. Matthew 6:20 tells us "But lay up for yourselves treasures in heaven, where neither moth nor rust destroys and where thieves do not break in and steal." Therefore, when we do good, we are storing treasures for ourselves in heaven. Don't let man stop us from doing good and rob us of our treasure. Amen! Praise God! Rejoice in the Lord Always!

DAY 211

"Everything is permissible"--- but not everything is beneficial. "Everything is permissible"--- but not everything is con-structive."

1 Corinthians 10:23 NIV

God gives us free will...freedom to make our own choices. Since most of the choices we make will affect our life, let us consult the right source. Let us consult God for anything big or small for He is our right source. God will give us the right answers that will lead us down the right path. Most of our actions will then be beneficial and constructive. Let us know that our choices not only affect us, but also others.

Therefore, before we act on something, let us consider the affect our action will have on others. Our actions may not be unlawful, but they may hurt and not be in the best interest of others or ourselves. Let us freely go to God and He will freely give us the right answers. Amen! Praise God! Rejoice in the Lord Always!

185

DAY 212

"For there is a proper time and procedure for every matter, though a man's misery weighs heavily upon him."
Ecclesiastes 8:6 NIV

We can't rush God! No matter what's going on in our life. We can't rush God for a solution to our problems, relief from our suffering, or answers to our prayers. God knows exactly what we are going through and He has already ordained a time for our blessing.

God has perfect timing and nothing is going to happen before His time. God wants us to hold on, be content, and find refuge in Him while we wait for our breakthrough. Being impatient and trying to take matters in our own hands will only lead to more misery.

God has a time for everything and everything is done according to His will and purpose, not ours. Let us lean on God while we wait upon Him. God is in control and great blessings come out of tough times. Amen! Praise God! Rejoice in the Lord Always!

DAY 213

"Not one word has failed of all the good promises He gave through his servant Moses."
1 Kings 8:56b NIV

We can literally take God at His Word. When God promises us something, we can believe He will make good on His promise. God says exactly what He means, and He means what He says. God cannot and will not lie. All the promises God has ever made, He has kept. So when God tells us that He will never leave us nor forsake us, we can believe He is with us forever.

The Bible will reveal to us all of God's promises that have come true for the people of Israel. And, the same promises that have come true for the people of Israel will come true for us today if we believe in God and His Word. We can trust and depend on God because He is a man of His Word. Amen! Praise God! Rejoice in the Lord Always!

DAY 214

"For it is by grace you have been saved, through faith and this not from yourselves, it is the gift of God not by works, so that no one can boast. For we are God's workmanship, created in Christ Jesus to do good works, which God prepared in advance for us to do."
Ephesians 2:8-10 NIV

Many of us think we have to get ourselves "right" before we come to accept Christ as our Lord and Savior. But let us know there is nothing we have to do or can do to prepare ourselves to accept Christ. God wants us to come to Him just as we are because we are saved by His grace and not by us doing or being good.

God will mold us into who He wants us to be after we open our heart and let Him into our life. Let us let God in because when God walks in, the devil walks out. Amen! Praise God! Rejoice in the Lord Always!

DAY 215

"Take my yoke upon you and learn from me, for I am gentle and humble in heart, and you will find rest for your souls. For my yoke is easy and my burden is light."
Matthew 11:29-30 NIV

Sometimes we may feel that our burdens are so heavy that we can't carry on. But, there is rest for our tired souls. Jesus is willing and able to carry all of our burdens. When we walk with Jesus, it becomes easier for us to turn over our burdens to Him.

Our burdens will continue to weigh us down when we don't hand them over. Our burdens are LIGHT with Jesus and they are TEMPORARY because troubles don't last always, and they are NECESSARY to build up our faith in Christ Jesus. Amen! Praise God! Rejoice in the Lord Always!

DAY 216

"Do not listen to Hezekiah, for he is misleading you when he says, 'The Lord will deliver us.'

2 Kings 18:32c NIV

Even though many people have seen the wonders of the Lord and believe, there are still some people that don't believe. The unbelievers will try to challenge our faith in the Lord so let's be strong in our faith and don't sway to the right or left. They will try to tell us what we believe the Lord can do is wrong. Therefore, when the unbelievers come

189

around, let us stay strong by remembering what the Lord has already done for us.

As believers, we can understand the things of God. The unbelievers are spiritually blind, walking around in the darkness and not able to understand. We were once blind, but now we see. Let us pray that one day all unbelievers will be able to open their eyes and see and understand "The Lord can deliver us." Amen! Praise God! Rejoice in the Lord Always!

DAY 217

"By faith the harlot Rahab did not perish with those who did not believe, when she received the spies with peace."
Hebrews 11:31 NIV

Let us walk by faith and not by sight. With God, we don't have to see it before we believe it. Faith is having confidence in God's ability to deliver on His promise. Rahab believed without seeing and her life was changed forever. She did not know God, but she heard about the things God was doing for His people and her faith grew. Rahab's faith in God gave her the courage to risk her life when she hid the spies and defied her King.

Rahab was a prostitute, but God used her because of her faith.

God can change our life and use us no matter what we did, as long as we are willing to believe in Him, step out on faith and trust Him. As long as we have faith in God, our life will never be the same. Reach for something in the darkness and absolutely trust God to put it in your hand. Amen! Praise God! Rejoice in the Lord Always!

DAY 218

"All these blessings will come upon you and accompany you if you obey the Lord your God: You will be blessed when you come in and blessed when you go out. The Lord will send a blessing on your barns and on everything you put your hand on.
Deuteronomy 28:2,6,8a NIV

In everything we do, we like to succeed and prosper and not fail. When we go on a diet, we follow many things to succeed and prosper, but none is guaranteed. When we go to work at a company, we want to be successful and prosper, but it is not guaranteed. However, when we follow and obey God, we can be successful and prosperous in all that we do and God can guarantee that.

God is the Master with the master plan. Let Him show us how to be successful and prosperous. God never fails. He always succeeds and prospers and that is guaranteed. Amen! Praise God! Rejoice in the Lord Always!

DAY 219

"Then saith He to the disciple, "Behold thy mother!"
John 19:27 KJV

As Jesus was dying on the cross, one of His last thoughts was not on Himself or His situation, but on His mother. Jesus loved His mother and was concerned about her welfare. Jesus asked John his disciple to care for His mother. Sometimes we need to forget about our circumstance and ourselves, and show love and celebrate our mother. Let us celebrate mothers on earth and the mothers that have gone home to be with the Lord.

A mother's love is special and it should never be forgotten or taken for granted. Mothers are a precious gift from God, so let us cherish and care for them. Let us give our heart to our mothers, for they have given us theirs. Amen! Praise God! Rejoice in the Lord Always!

DAY 220

"So then, those who suffer according to God's will should commit themselves to their faithful Creator and continue to do good."
1 Peter 4:19 NIV

None of us like to suffer, but suffering is a part of life. All of us will suffer several times throughout our lifetime. However, let us count our suffering for God's will all joy. God always has a purpose for our suffering. God does not make us suffer just to see us suffer. In our suffering, God has a lesson for us to learn that will allow us to draw closer to Him, make us a better person, and make life more joyful.

Let us pray for spiritual understanding so God's lessons can be revealed to us. Let us continue to trust and depend on God for He is still with us as we suffer. Suffering is something God intends for us to go through and not be stuck in. Let us always hold onto and never let go of God's unchanging hands. Amen! Praise God! Rejoice in the Lord Always!

DAY 221

"For you created my inmost being; you knit me together in my mother's womb. I praise you because I am fearfully and wonderfully made; your works are wonderful, I know that full well."

Psalm 139:13-14 NIV

We are all special from the time of conception. God created us unique, yet similar in many ways. God sees us all equal, and no one is better than the other. Let us stand tall with confidence knowing that God loves us and we are "fearfully and wonderfully made." God does not create any junk or make mistakes.

Each one of us was created to serve the Lord and live according to His will and purpose. We are all special and don't let nobody else tell us otherwise. God sees the best in us even when we don't see it in ourselves. Amen! Praise God! Rejoice in the Lord Always!

DAY 222

"The Lord your God himself will drive them out of your way."

Joshua 23:5 NIV

194

When our enemies rise up against us, we do not need an army to win the battle. All we need is the Lord. No matter what situation we are in the Lord is always by our side. The Lord does not want us to fight evil with evil. The Lord wants us to allow Him to fight our battles. The Lord fought for the Israelites and He will fight for us. The Lord is stronger then all of our enemies and He will defeat them all of the time.

So when our enemies start calling us names, gossiping about us or want to cause us harm, let us remain calm and remember the Lord "will drive them out of our way." The battle is not ours, it's the Lord's. Amen! Praise God! Rejoice in the Lord Always!

DAY 223

"At my first defense no one stood with me, but all forsook me. May it not be charged against them."
2 Timothy 4:16 NKJV

We can't put our confidence in man because man is limited in what he can do. And we can't get mad when man let us down because God made man not to be totally dependable. God wants us to put our confidence in Him and totally depend on Him only. If man were very dependable, we would not seek God. So let us recognize that we need to depend on God because He is the only one that we can rely on to come to our defense.

Let us rely on God to supply all of our needs, rely on Him for strength, rely on Him for healing, and rely on Him for everything. Jeremiah 17:7 tells us "But blessed is the man who trusts in the Lord, whose confidence is in him." Let us be blessed! God is faithful even when we are unfaithful. Amen! Praise God! Rejoice in the Lord Always!

DAY 224

"And pray in the Spirit on all occasions with all kinds of prayers and requests."
Ephesians 6:18 NIV

Prayer is powerful; it changes people and situations. So if we want change let us pray continually. Let us stop making excuses for reasons why we can't pray. We can pray a short or long prayer. We can pray anytime day or night in our homes, jobs, cars, trains, bus, standing, sitting, bowing, anywhere and any place. God wants to hear from us. God hears and answers our prayers; He may not give us the answer we want, but He knows best.

Prayer is talking to God. The more we talk to God, the closer we draw to Him. Prayer is the key to change and our faith that God hears our prayers and we will receive unlocks the door. Amen! Praise God! Rejoice in the Lord Always!

DAY 225

"Therefore we do not lose heart. Though outwardly we are wasting away, yet inwardly we are being renewed day by day."
2 Corinthians 4:16 NIV

Let us continue daily to have hope and a cheerful heart despite what is going on in our personal life and around us. It is easy to quit and give up when we focus on our problems and not God. Even though our outer body is wasting away, the Spirit of God is renewing our inner spirit with strength day by day.

Let us walk with God instead of walking away. With God, we can continue to forge ahead and face any problem that comes our way. Amen! Praise God! Rejoice in the Lord Always!

DAY 226

"Peter and the other apostles replied: "We must obey God rather than men!"
Acts 5:29 NIV

God, not man, knows the road we need to travel on in order to have a wonderful and joyful life. God, not man, has the instructions we need to obey and follow in order to have safe travel along that road. God, not man, knows what to do when we come face to face with trouble along that road.

We might not know our destination along that road, but we know with God we will get there. God is our ultimate source. Man cannot think nor do what God does. Let us allow God to be our travel guide so He can lead us to a place where no man can. Amen! Hallelujah! Rejoice in the Lord Always!

DAY 227

"If you make the Most High your dwelling-even the Lord, who is my refuge- then no harm will befall you, no disaster will come near your tent. For he will command his angels concerning you to guard you in all ways; they will lift you up in their hands, so that you will not strike your foot against a stone."

Psalm 91:9-12 NIV

It is good to have someone to run to when we need protection and safety. The Lord strong and mighty is our protector. He will rescue us from all harm and danger. In times of trouble, God will dispatch His angels to protect us.

God won't let us stumble or fall. Let us trust the Lord and know He will be there when we need Him. Amen! Praise God for His protection! Rejoice in the Lord Always!

DAY 228

"Do not repay evil with evil or insult with insult, but with blessing, because to this you were called so that you may inherit a blessing."

1 Peter 3:9 NIV

Let us not allow others to dictate how we will act. We give them power over us and allow them to steal our blessing and joy when we try to get revenge. When we are confronted with evil, God wants us to continue to do good and pray for those who are evil and wicked.

Let us not block our flow of blessings by imitating the evil one. We are living to please God, not man. Amen! Praise God for his blessings! Rejoice in the Lord Always!

DAY 229

"Do not grieve, for the joy of the Lord is your strength."

Nehemiah 8:10c NIV

Let us enjoy and be happy for life is too short for us to worry and grieve over our problems, or what should have been, or what we did or did not do. Sometimes we give our problems too much attention and we let them steal our joy. We should be enjoying life instead of worrying about it. We can't change or do anything about most of the things we worry about, so why worry. God created this world and everything in it for us to enjoy.

We can only truly enjoy life if we put our trust in the Lord and rely on Him to solve our problems. When we worry, we are telling God we don't trust in His ability to solve our problems. We might not be able to solve our problems, but God can. Let us give our problems to the Lord in prayer and get our joy back. Laugh, Smile, Enjoy! Amen! Praise God! Rejoice in the Lord Always!

DAY 230

"The Lord is my shepherd; I shall not want. He makes me to lie down in green pastures; He leads me beside the still waters. He restores my soul; He leads in the path of righteousness for His name's sake."
Psalm 23:1-3 NKJV

We can totally depend on the Lord as sheep totally depends on the shepherd. The Lord is our "Good Shepherd" and we are His sheep. The Lord provides all that we need and we shall not want. As the sheep depends on his shepherd for provisions, guidance and protection, we too can depend on the Lord for these things. Sheep will not lie down in green pastures or be led by water until they are without fear.

Well, we can release our fear and find safety, peace and rest when we put our faith in the Lord and allow Him to be our refuge. Trusting in the Lord will restore our soul. Let us allow the Lord to lead us to the right place in the right way for His Glory for the Lord is our Shepherd. Amen! Praise God! Rejoice in the Lord Always!

DAY 231

"May the Lord repay you for what you have done. May you be richly rewarded by the Lord, the God of Israel, under whose wings you have come to take refuge."
Ruth 2:12 NIV

The things we do for others and the way we do them say a lot about who we are as a person. When we sacrifice ourselves for the benefit of others and exhibit kindness, love, generosity, patience and loyalty, we develop a good reputation. A good reputation is a valuable asset pleasing to God and man, and it is built from possessing a strong moral character. A good reputation honors God and He is glorified in our actions.

The good we do for others comes back to us. God blesses us when we bless others. Let us sacrifice ourselves for others as the Lord sacrificed Himself for us. Amen! Praise God! Rejoice in the Lord Always!

DAY 232

"Then He arose and rebuked the wind, and said to the sea, "Peace, be still!" And the wind ceased and there was a great calm."
Mark 4:39 NIV

We can make it through any storm with hope and faith in Jesus Christ. Jesus has the power to calm any storm that we might go through. Jesus is much more powerful than any storm and everything obeys His commands. Some storms are longer and stronger than others, creating many losses. These losses may be to our finances, health, job, home, or loved one.

No matter what type of storm or how many losses we might face, let us know we can come out of it on the other side with victory, peace and joy. We have a friend in Jesus in all of our sorrows, losses and grief He will bear. In every life, some rain must fall to help us grow. Amen! Praise God! Rejoice in the Lord Always!

DAY 233

"Behold, I have refined you, but not as silver; I have tested you in the furnace of affliction."
Isaiah 48:10 NKJV

Let us know God is only testing us when we face trials of any kind. Through our afflictions, God is transforming and elevating us to a higher level in Him. God is teaching us how to depend on Him, trust Him, have faith in Him and grow in His image. So let us hold on and be strong through the storm, for it is only a test. We can pass the test! God won't test us any further than we can withstand.

In the end, after we have passed the test God has promised to give us, the ultimate reward is "the crown of life." At heaven's gate, God will say "Well done, good and faithful servant." Studying the Bible will help us to pass the test. Amen! Praise God! Rejoice in the Lord Always!

DAY 234

"But Paul, greatly annoyed, turned and said to the spirit, "I command you in the name of Jesus Christ to come out of her." And he came out that very hour."
Acts 16:18b NKJV

Jesus has given us the power and authority over demons. We have the power and authority to take back everything and everyone we have ever lost to the devil. We no longer have to feel hopeless and powerless. We have the power and all we need to do is claim it "In the Name of Jesus Christ."

We have the power and authority to take back our children, spouse, parents, finances, and job, home anything or anyone we have ever lost to the devil. We are saved today because someone used their power and authority to take us back.

So let us claim our power and authority and speak life, success and prosperity over the lives of our love ones and our life. There is Life Changing Power in the name of Jesus Christ. The lost can be found. Amen! Praise God! Rejoice in the Lord Always!

DAY 235

"Give thanks to the God of heaven."

Psalm 136:26 NIV

Let us give thanks to God for being our Healer. God is our Healer and He will heal us when we are broken. He makes us whole and He makes it possible for us to claim our joy again. If we are walking around broken, we are just living to survive, not thriving, and fully enjoying life to its fullest. Let us know God will heal our broken heart, spirit, soul, health, finances, relationship, bones, promises and disappointments.

We never ever have to stay sick and walk around broken. Let us not hold it inside whatever is broken and needs mending, but let us pick up the broken pieces and take them to the Lord in prayer. We might not be able to fix our problem, but the Lord can.

There is nothing the Lord can't fix. He has the power. God gave us His only begotten Son and Jesus Christ suffered on the cross so that we might be healed. When we get tired of being sick, let us call onto the Lord. He is our Healer and only He can help us pick up the pieces and make us whole. Thank You Lord for the healing. Amen! Praise God! Rejoice the Lord Always!

DAY 236

"For the Lord your God is a merciful God; He will not abandon or destroy you or forget the covenant with your forefathers, which He confirmed to them by oath."

Deuteronomy 4:31 NIV

We can always count on the Lord our God to be there for us. God promises to never abandon or destroy us. So no matter what we have done, we can always go before the Lord and ask for forgiveness. We serve a merciful God and there is nothing we can do that He will not forgive.

God won't abandon or destroy us because we sinned. We abandon God when we don't ask for forgiveness. God knows it is common for man to sin and that we will never be sinless, but he wants us to strive to sin less.

We all fall down, but it is the strong who gets back up. When we get back up, God is there waiting for us with open arms every time. Everywhere we go, He is there. He is guiding and directing so that we won't stumble nor fall. Let us not abandon God, because He won't abandon us. Amen! Praise God! Rejoice in the Lord Always!

DAY 237

"Do not love the world or the things in the world. If anyone loves the world, the love of the Father is not in him."

1 John 2:15 NKJV

Let us not allow Satan to lead us astray. Satan is the leader and organizer of the world and the things in the world. Satan wants us to stay in love with the world and follow him. Therefore, Satan is going to tempt us with things that are pleasing to the flesh so it will be harder for us to leave.

However, we can overcome the world and walk away. We can't do it on our own, but we can do it with strength and guidance from the Lord. When we don't have light on a dark road, we can go down the wrong road, lose our way, and stumble and fall.

If we keep our mind on things that are of God, we can break that hold the world has on us. If we want to really enjoy life and have some real fun, let us stop hanging out with Satan and hang out with the Father. Satan is not our real friend, God is. Love God! Amen! Praise God! Rejoice in the Lord Always!

DAY 238

"I will maintain my righteousness and never let go of it; my conscience will not reproach me as long as I live."

Job 27:6 NIV

Let us maintain our integrity at all times. We can't allow others or our circumstances to dictate how we will act. We don't have to respond ungodly because someone or our circumstance made us angry. When we respond ungodly, we are giving them way too much power by allowing them to control our behavior and change our character. Psalm 4:4 tells us "Be angry, and do not sin. Meditate within your heart on your bed, and be still."

So let us pray to God, consult our heart, and find the best way to respond. We can continue to walk right, talk right and do right despite our anger. Job maintained his righteousness despite what his friends were saying and despite his circumstances because he loved God more. Amen! Praise God! Rejoice in the Lord Always!

DAY 239

"Now there was also a dispute among them, as to which of them should be considered the greatest."

Luke 22:24 NKJV

Sometimes in our homes, at church and on our jobs, there are too many people wanting to be chiefs and not Indians. Too many people want to consider themselves the greatest. However, there is only one person who is truly the greatest and that is Jesus Christ. Jesus Christ is all knowing and all-powerful and there is nobody greater.

So let us come before Jesus humbly as a servant and be content in whatever position we are in. Jesus has us in a position where our Spiritual Gifts could be the most effective. Jesus Christ sees us all equal; everybody and every job is important.

When Jesus Christ wants us to be promoted to another level, He will promote us. When we try to change our own status, Jesus is nowhere in it. Let us allow Jesus to be the head of our life for He is the greatest. Amen! Praise God! Rejoice in the Lord Always!

DAY 240

"Your word is a lamp to my feet and a light to my path."

Psalm 119:105 NKJV

The Bible is God's word...inspired by God. The Bible is very powerful and it is important for us to know the Bible as we journey through life. The more we read and understand the Bible, the more we know and understand life. The Bible helps us to understand God, our life, our purpose, and our destiny. Life's journey can be very confusing and difficult, and living without the Word of God is like walking down a dark road at night without any light.

When we don't have light on a dark road, we can go down the wrong road, lose our way, and stumble and fall. The light helps us to stay on the right road and it shows us what is lurking in the darkness. The Bible still remains the number one Best Seller among all books. Let us pick up the Bible today so God can show us the way to a "better life." Amen! Praise God! Rejoice in the Lord Always!

DAY 241

"Now to Him who is able to do exceedingly abundantly above all that we ask or think, according to the power that works in us,"
                    Ephesians 3:20 NKJV

Let us continually praise the Lord from whom all blessings flow and to whom we owe our thanks. God is able to give us much more than we ever can pray for more than we ever can conceive. There are no bounds to which God can bless us. Let us go before the Lord in prayer, ask for more, and expect more. Let us not put any limits to what the Lord can do for us. Be encouraged by what the Lord has already done.

In 1 Samuel 1, Hannah was grieved because she was barren and wanted a child. In verse 11, Hannah took her sorrows to the Lord in prayer and prayed for a male child. The Lord not only blessed her with the male child she prayed for, He blessed her with three sons and two daughters. Hannah was faithful to the Lord and she believed. The Lord will do for us what He has already done for others. Trust God! Amen! Praise God! Rejoice in the Lord Always!

DAY 242

"And the Lord said to Satan, "The Lord rebuke you, Satan!"
Zechariah 3:2 NKJV

Sometimes we also need to say "Rebuke you Satan!" Satan prowls around trying to destroy us. Satan does not want us to receive what God has planned for us. The closer we get to God, the more Satan attacks us.

Let us tell Satan he is a liar and tell him he cannot have our family, friends or us! Let us call on the Lord for strength and guidance so we can resist the devil, then he will flee. Amen! Rejoice in the Lord Always!

DAY 243

"We have not received the spirit of the world but the Spirit of who is from God, that we may understand what God has freely given us."
1 Corinthians 2:12 NIV

When Jesus went to sit at the right hand of God, He sent us the Holy Spirit to dwell within us and guide us into an intimate relationship with God. Through the power and guidance of the Holy Spirit, we can begin to understand God and His Word. As the Holy

213

Spirit guides us, He will reveal to us the thoughts and actions of Christ. We will be able to talk to God and recognize His small voice whispering to us. Through the Holy Spirit, we will begin to know and understand what God's good and perfect will is for us.

Thank you God for giving us the guidance and power of the Holy Spirit so that we may have a closer walk with thee. Amen! Praise God! Rejoice in the Lord Always!

DAY 244

"Judge not, that ye be not judged."
Matthew 7:1 KJV

We hate to be judged, but we love to judge everyone else. We love to point out what is wrong with others and what is so right with ourselves. However with the same measure we judge others, we also will be judged. We should pray for others instead of judging them.

Prayer is the best thing we can do for others. We don't know everyone's story and why they do or wear such things. They may wear flip-flops to church, because that is all they can afford.

Only God is perfect. Let us not ignore the plank in our own eye and see the speck in our

214

brother's eye. Let us spread love, instead of venom and gossip. God calls us to Love thy neighbor as thy self. Amen! Hallelujah! Rejoice in the Lord Always!

DAY 245

"When she heard about Jesus, she came behind Him in the crowd and touched His garment. For she said, "If only I may touch His clothes, I shall be made well."
Mark 5:27-28 NKJV

This woman in the scripture had an issue with bleeding for twelve years. She was sick for a long time and could have given up all hope of being healed. However, she didn't. She kept her faith and hope alive in Christ Jesus.

She heard about Jesus and she knew what He could do. She knew that only Jesus had the power to take away her afflictions and make her whole again. Let us never give up no matter how long we have been suffering.

Let us also keep our faith and hope alive in Christ Jesus, and remember what He can do. Jesus is a healer. He can restore our body, soul and spirit. Let us have the courage to seek the Lord and the determination to wait upon Him. Our faith can make us well. Amen! Praise God! Rejoice in the Lord Always!

DAY 246

"He heals the brokenhearted and binds up their wounds."

Psalm 147:3 NKJV

We may face many different rejections in our lifetime. We may be rejected from a love one, a relative, a friend or a business partner. Whatever rejections we may face, let us remember there is a reason and season for people and places. God has people coming and going in our life for a reason. And when we try to hold on to what God wants us to let go, we miss our blessing.

Everyone serves a purpose, and now is their time to move on. Rejections may hurt and our hearts may be broken, but God can mend a broken heart. Let us give our heart to God! Amen! Praise God! Rejoice in the Lord Always!

DAY 247

"May the God of hope fill you with all joy and peace as you trust in Him, so that you may overflow with hope by the power of the Holy Spirit."

Romans 15:13 NIV

Let us trust in the Lord so that we may be filled with real joy, true peace and overflow with hope. With all the things that are troubling many of us these days, we need joy, peace and hope in order to make it through another day. Trusting in the Lord quiets our soul and gives joy to our heart.

Hope helps us to endure the pain of hardship and helps us to persevere in spite of our difficulties. Joy, peace and hope are essential ingredients for true happiness and they can only be found when we trust in the Lord.

Let us trust in the Lord and uncover the ingredients to true happiness. Let us trust the Lord not man because nobody can do us like the Lord. TRUST is only five letters, but it is a big word. Amen! Praise God! Rejoice in the Lord Always!

DAY 248

"If you abide in Me, and My words abide in you, you will ask what you desire, and it shall be done for you."

John 15:7 NKJV

We don't have to chase the wind or sell our souls for material gains. We are the children of the Most High God and He will shower us with the finer things of His creation. Our Father owns all of the glorious riches in the world and He wants us to enjoy them.

God will not only provide all we need, He will also give us things that we desire. All God wants us to do in order to receive such great gifts is to be obedient to Him and follow in His ways. When we are obedient to God, all we have to do is "Ask and it shall be given to us."

Our obedience lets God know that when He gives us the finer things of His creation, they will be used for His glory and not our own selfish gain. Things given to us by God will last forever. Let us chase God and not the wind! Amen! Praise God! Rejoice in the Lord Always!

DAY 249

"God is our refuge and strength, a very present help in trouble.'
                                    Psalm 46:1 NKJV

Let us know without a doubt that when trouble is surrounding us, so is God. We can depend on God to be there to save us when we need Him the most. In times of trouble, we can give God all of our tears, pain, weakness, stress and burdens. For God is our comforter and He will wipe away all of our tears. God is our healer and He will take away all of our pain.

When we are weak, we are strong for God will give us strength in our times of weakness. God is our peace giver and He will take away all of our stress. God is our deliverer and He will deliver us from all of our burdens and give us rest. God is our refuge and we can depend on Him from now until eternity.

When we see one set of footprints in the sand, they are not ours. They belong to the Lord for those are the times when He is carrying us. Call on God! Amen! Praise God! Rejoice in the Lord Always!

DAY 250

"Gideon said to Him, "O my lord, if the Lord is with us, why then has all this happened to us?"

Judges 6:13a NKJV

Unfortunately, life is going to throw us some curve balls that will cause us to become discouraged and question, "If the Lord is really with us" and "why then is this happening." However, let us not become discouraged. Life is going to be with its share of troubles and the Lord will be with us as we come face to face with them all.

We will suffer in our lifetime for many different reasons. One reason is that we ourselves will cause our own trouble by following someone other than God. Then sometimes God will test us so we can grow spiritually and other times God will punish us for our disobedience.

Satan comes with trouble and dumps it right in our lap. If we stay in prayer, God will tell us why our suffering comes. We can have the victory over all of our troubles because the Lord is always by our side. Be encouraged, trouble doesn't last always. Amen! Praise God! Rejoice in the Lord Always!

DAY 251

"If the world hates you, you know that it hated Me before it hated you."

John 15:18 NKJV

Not everyone is going to be happy about the work we are doing for the Lord. Some people are going to try to stop us from doing the Lord's work with jealously, hatred, envy and gossip. But let us not grow weary doing good for the Lord, for in due time we shall all reap what we sow. If we sow love, we will reap love. If we sow hate, we will reap hate. So, when some people spread hate, let us be like Jesus and spread love.

Jesus had many haters and He kept on spreading love and doing the Father's work despite it all. We are here to please God, not man! Let us not allow our haters to deter us from the plan that God has for us. Let us push on anyhow! Amen! Praise God! Rejoice in the Lord Always!

DAY 252

"Now the Lord came and stood and called as at other times, "Samuel! Samuel!" And Samuel answered, "Speak, for your servant hears."

1 Samuel 3:10 NKJV

REJOICE: A Celebration of Life

Let us take time out of our busy schedule daily and steal away to a quiet place so we can listen for the small voice of the Lord calling us. The Lord wants to tell us many things, many things we never heard before. The Lord wants to tell us about the plans He has for our life.

He wants to give us instructions on how to live a joyful life. He wants to give us the answers to our problems. He wants to tell us who our enemies are; and most of all, He wants to tell us He loves us. But we will not know these things and we will miss many blessings if we don't take time out and listen for the voice of the Lord.

Let us not allow anything or anyone to get in our way of communicating with the Lord. Lord, please block out all outside noise so we can hear you and only you speak. In Jesus name, we pray. Amen! Praise God! Rejoice in the Lord Always!

DAY 253

"But our citizenship is in heaven."
Philippians 3:20 NIV

Where Christ resides, we as believers shall reside there too. We belong to Christ so one day we will leave this place and live eternally in heaven with Christ. We will trade

222

our human body for a spiritual body and live in union with Christ. So let us prepare ourselves for our heavenly dwelling by being an imitator of Christ. Even though we live here on earth, we are to take on Christ-like values. Christ calls us to act more like Him, and not like the world.

Just because we live in this world, it doesn't mean we have to act as the world does. Therefore, let us be like Christ and clothe ourselves with love, kindness, forgiveness, gentleness, self-control, patience, goodness, and faithfulness. Let us imitate Christ for we are made in His image. Amen! Praise God! Rejoice in the Lord Always!

DAY 254

"So David said to God, "I have sinned greatly, because I have done this thing; but now, I pray, take away the iniquity of Your servant, for I have done very foolishly."
1 Chronicles 21:8 NKJV

God knows when we sin; He sees what we are doing at all times. We might be able to hide our sins from other people, but we can't hide them from God. Even though God knows all about our sins, He wants us to go before Him, admit what we did was wrong, take full

223

responsibility for them and ask for forgiveness.

We can't right our wrongs unless we realize we have done something wrong, sorry for it and willing to change to do it no more. We can change and live the life God called us to live. We don't have to do this alone.

The Holy Spirit living inside of us will help us realize our wrongs and help guide us in the right direction. If we go before God with a changed heart, confessing our sins, He will forgive our sins and remember them no more. We serve a Merciful God! Amen! Praise God! Rejoice in the Lord Always!

DAY 255

"But my God shall supply all your need according to His riches in glory by Christ Jesus."

Philippians 4:19 KJV

We don't have to worry about where our next meal is coming from or how our bills will be paid or where will we get strength. Our Father in heaven is watching over us. He knows what we need and when we need it. No matter what it is we need, God shall supply it. We might not get all we want, but we will surely get all we need.

God is great. He takes care of us better then we take care of ourselves. "Look at the birds of the air; they neither sow nor reap nor gather into barns, and yet your heavenly Father feeds them. Are you not of more value than they?" (Matthew 6:26) Let us not worry, let us trust God! Amen! Praise God! Rejoice in the Lord Always!

DAY 256

"No weapon that is formed against you shall prosper;"

Isaiah 54:17 KJV

Let us not be fearful or discouraged we are not in this battle alone. God is on our side. He is our sword and shield. God is on our front line ready to fight our battles. Our foes and adversity might rise up against us, but they will not succeed. With God on our side, we will always prevail with truth and victory.

At times it might seem like our foes and adversity are winning against us, but let us hold on to our faith and hope and never let go, because just at the right time God steps in. Mighty and powerful is God. We can depend on Him to protect us physically and spiritually in times of trouble, harm, and danger. With God, our battles are already won. Amen! Praise God! Rejoice in the Lord Always!

DAY 257

"The angel said to those who were standing before him, "Take off his filthy clothes." Then he said to Joshua, "See, I have taken away your sin, and I will put fine garments on you."
Zechariah 3:4 NIV

Let us come in the presence of the Lord just as we are filthy clothes and all. For only the Lord can clean us up and turn our life around. Many times people will say, "I have to clean myself up before I go to the Lord," but if we wait until we clean ourselves up we will never go before the Lord. We can't clean ourselves the way the Lord can. The Lord will exchange our old filthy garments for a fine rich robe; one which money can't buy.

Just imagine being clothed by the Lord in all His righteousness. Jesus came to take away the sins of the world; let us make sure ours are included. Amen! Praise God! Rejoice in the Lord Always!

DAY 258

"Then he showed me Joshua the high priest standing before the angel of the Lord, and Satan standing at his right side to accuse him."

Zechariah 3:1 NIV

Satan stands before us ready to accuse and destroy us, but God stands before us protecting us from Satan's attacks. Satan hates when we are in the presence of God because he then knows that we have a great protector and defender on our side. God fights our spiritual battles. He does not allow Satan just to have his way with us.

Just like with Job, God regulates what Satan can do to us and He does not put on us more then we can bear. So the next time we feel we are being attacked, remember the Lord knows all about it. It is only a test. We are ready for battle because the Lord is on our side. Let us stand firm in the Lord because He stands firm with us. Amen! Praise God! Rejoice in the Lord Always!

DAY 259

"And he said unto them, Go ye into all the world, and preach the gospel to every creature."

Mark 16:15 KJV

How do we expect people to hear about the goodness of God and all He has done for us if we keep what God has done for us to ourselves. In the Bible, Rehab the harlot, the woman who had issues with bleeding and many others came to know the Lord and their life was changed only after hearing about the goodness of the Lord from other people.

The Lord is good and He has blessed us over and over again. We can't keep this kind of good news to ourselves. We have to spread it, shout it out, and tell the whole world about it.

Telling others about the goodness of the Lord is better than giving them silver or gold. Silver or gold might lose its luster or value, but the Word of God changes lives for eternity. Share the good news about the Lord and give someone an opportunity to have a better life. Amen! Praise God! Rejoice in the Lord Always!

DAY 260

"But if ye do not forgive, neither will your Father which is in heaven forgive your trespasses."

Mark 11:26 KJV

In our lifetime we will meet some people who will do us wrong and make us angry. And when they do, God calls us to pray and forgive them. No matter how many people do us wrong or make us angry, God wants us to forgive them each and every time.

We want to be forgiven by God and others, but we find it very difficult to forgive others for the things they do to us. We want to hold on to the hurt, curse them or get revenge, but this is no way to live because eventually, we allow them to steal our joy.

Harboring unforgiveness can cause us physical and emotional pain. We don't go places where someone we can't forgive is because we are unhappy when they are happy. We are stuck in the past while they move on with their future. Let us pray to God and ask Him to teach us how to forgive. When we forgive, it leaves room for God's wrath. Amen! Praise God! Rejoice in the Lord Always!

DAY 261

"Be anxious for nothing, but in everything by prayer and supplication, with thanksgiving, let your requests be made known to God; and the peace of God, which surpasses all understanding, will guard your hearts and minds through Christ Jesus."

Philippians 4:6-7 NKJV

We all become anxious about something. And we try our best to take our mind off whatever is bothering us, but our mind keeps thinking about them. We don't have to be anxious anymore and our mind can be free to think on the good things. We serve an awesome God who can take away our anxieties. He can do what we can't. When anxiety overtakes us, let us not fall apart, but fall down on our knees, pray, and trust God to work things out.

Prayer is the outpouring of the soul and supplication is stating our wants. We must always come to God in thanksgiving, not in a complaining spirit, but with thankfulness for present mercies (People's New Testament). Let us give our problems to the Lord. He can do something about them. Amen! Praise God! Rejoice in the Lord Always!

DAY 262

"The Lord will fulfill his purpose for me; your love, O Lord, endures forever--- do not abandon the works of your hands."
Psalm 138:8 NIV

We are not here on earth by chance; God planned for our existence. God created us because He has something great planned for us to do. With God, we are destined for greatness. Let us know the Lord has begun His great works in us and He will continue His great works in us eternally. God will continue His great works in us despite our fault, because He loves us and only sees the best in us.

And whatever God has planned for us is for us and no man can take it away. Man might try to throw obstacles in our way, but God will just take us above, underneath, around or through them. There is no stopping God! Let us hold onto God's unchanging hands and let us allow Him to lead us to greatness. Amen! Praise God! Rejoice in the Lord Always!

DAY 263

"Keep your tongue from evil and lips from speaking lies."

Psalm 34:13 NIV

Sometimes we think it is better to tell a lie then the truth. But, it is never better to lie. "A little white lie" is no better than a big lie. God sees any and all lies as a sin. When we try to fix something with a lie, we push God right out the picture. God is not in the midst of any situation that involves lies or deceit. When we lie, we are telling God we have the ability to fix our own situation and He does not.

God can fix any and all situations no matter how bad it may appear to us. God can do all things, but fail. Let us trust God to fix any and all of our situations because lies or deceit has never fixed anything. Speak the truth and the truth shall set you free. Amen! Praise God! Rejoice in the Lord Always!

DAY 264

"It is for freedom that Christ has set us free."
Galatians 5:1 NIV

We are free indeed. We are free; no longer in bondage. Christ has come and given us our freedom. He broke the chains that once held us captive. It feels good to be free. With Christ comes freedom. Hallelujah!

We are free from the hold Satan had on us. We are free to love. We are free to expect favor and blessings from God. We are free to know everything will turn out for our good. We are free to know we can do all things through Christ who strengthens us.

We are free to have hope and faith. We are free to trust and depend on God. We are free to know God will provide. We are free to know God will give us the victory. We are free to receive grace and mercy. We are free to know God is with us and He will never leave us. We are free to reap what we sow. We are free! Free indeed! Amen! Praise God! Rejoice in the Lord Always!

DAY 265

"God is with us; he is our leader."
2 Chronicles 13:12 NIV

God is with us for a purpose. God wants us to allow Him to be the head of our life and for us to seek Him for advice on things big or small. So we too can be victorious, overcome the world, and live a joyful life rich with blessings, grace and mercy now and for eternity.

God is the only one qualified to lead and guide us through this ever-changing world, full of things seen and unforeseen. God is all-knowing, all-powerful, and has everything and everyone in His presence.

We can trust God to lead and guide us down the right road to righteousness. We can't do it ourselves, so let us allow God to be our leader. God will lead us to places we have never been before. For a life of joy, peace, success and prosperity, follow God. If we follow, God will lead. Amen! Praise God! Rejoice in the Lord Always!

DAY 266

"I will bless the Lord at all times; His praise shall continually be in my mouth."
Psalm 34:1 NKJV

Let all the servants of the Lord lift their hands and Praise Him! Praise the Lord morning, noon and night. Meditate on His goodness. The Lord is so good to us. He is worthy of our praise. Where would we be if it had not been for the Lord on our side?

Praise the Lord for His endless love that never fails. It is the Lord who brings us through our difficult times. It is the Lord who puts food on our table, clothes on our back and shelter over our head. Praise the Lord for His kindness.

The Lord is one that blesses us, heals us, answers our prayers, and performs miracles. The Lord is the one who fights our battles and gives us the victory. Praise the Lord for His greatness. Let us open our heart and praise the Lord for all He has, is and will do for us. Praise the Lord for His grace and mercy. Amen! Praise God! Rejoice in the Lord Always!

DAY 267

"She said to Him, "Yes, Lord I believe that You are the Christ, the Son of God, who is to come into the world."
John 11:27 NKJV

"For God so loved the world that He gave us His only begotten Son, that whoever believes in Him should not perish but have everlasting life" (John 3:16). If we believe, we shall receive.

We shall receive eternal life and the goodness God has in store for us. God has a plan for our life, but we can't receive it unless we believe in the Son of God. Jesus, the Son of God is real, what He does is real and what He says is real. We can't see Jesus, but we can feel His presence.

We can see His miracles, wonderful deeds and marvelous works. We can hear His small voice. We can see the results of His blessings and answered prayers. Jesus is real!! Believe and receive. Lord please help our unbelief. Amen! Praise God! Rejoice in the Lord Always!

DAY 268

"And the God of all grace, who called you to his eternal glory in Christ, after you have suffered a little while, will himself restore you and make you strong, firm and steadfast."
1 Peter 5:10 NIV

Nobody enjoys suffering and many wish we never had to experience it. But it is inevitable that we will all suffer several times in our lifetime. Suffering does not have to be looked upon as a "bad thing" happening to us. In reality suffering can be considered a "good thing."

When we have suffered a little while, God restores us and then we tend to be wiser, more knowledgeable, stronger, developed a close relationship with Christ, have increased faith, more hope, and blessed. We will probably never know God or acquire many of these traits if we never suffer.

Let us remember, "It is in the valley where we grow." God is with us as we go through our suffering, He will never leave nor forsake us, abandon nor destroy us, and God can turn the bad into good. So in reality, suffering can be a "good thing." Amen! Praise God! Rejoice in the Lord Always!

DAY 269

"Jesus wept."

John 11:35 NKJV

Let us be comforted in our times of grief and sorrow knowing that Jesus weeps with us. Jesus weeps with us because He is full of compassion and love for us. Jesus hates to see us suffering and He knows the hurt and pain we go through because He Himself suffered more than we could ever imagine. If we call out to Jesus, He will restore our joy and end our suffering by giving us strength, encouragement, hope, faith and a human touch from others.

We can find peace and calmness through Jesus and in His Word during our times of grief and sorrow. "Weeping may endure for a night, but joy comes in the morning" (Psalm 30:5). Jesus cares. Amen! Praise God! Rejoice in the Lord Always!

DAY 270

"Open my eyes that I may see wonderful things in your law."

Psalm 119:18 NIV

Let us pray to God and ask Him to open our eyes so we can see all of His goodness. God has so many wonderful things to offer us so that we can have a great and rewarding life, but we have to open our eyes to see it. If we open our eyes, we can see and begin to strive for the things God has to offer. Many of us tend to see only a few good things God has to offer and not the whole picture. But the whole picture tells the whole story.

Let us take off our spiritual blinders, see the wonderful things of God, and know they are not there to restrict us from having a good time. Our good times will restrict us from living our best life. God is good and what He has to offer us is good. Amen! Praise God! Rejoice in the Lord Always!

DAY 271

"Do not be afraid though briers and thorns are all around you and you live among scorpions."
Ezekiel 2:6b NIV

When we find ourselves in a difficult situation or around difficult people, let us not be afraid for the hand of the Lord is upon us. The Lord has His hand stretched out for us to take a hold of during our most difficult times. The Lord will not leave us to battle our difficult times alone. Let us take hold of the Lord's hand so He can empower us with strength to stand firm and not fall during our difficult times.

We can stand firm and know that with God, all of our difficult situations will turn out for our good and all of our enemies will fall. Let us have faith and trust in the Lord for only He can rescue us from anything or anyone. Nobody is Greater. Keep the faith! Amen! Praise God! Rejoice in the Lord Always!

DAY 272

"Do not let any unwholesome talk come out of your mouths, but only what is helpful for building others up according to their needs, that it may benefit those who listen."
Ephesians 4:29 NIV

Our tongue can be our greatest asset or greatest liability. Our mothers always said if you could not say something nice, do not say anything at all. Apparently, God feels the same way. Controlling our tongue begins on the inside with our thinking process. If we keep our mind on Christ, we will speak Christ-like.

Let us be compassionate towards one another, say something nice to somebody and let us build each one up with love in Christ Jesus. We glorify God with our actions when we are nice to someone. As we bless others, someone will bless us. Amen! Hallelujah! Rejoice in the Lord Always!

DAY 273

"Let us hold unswervingly to the hope we profess, for he who is promised is faithful."
Hebrews 10:23 NIV

240

Let us not allow our hope to waiver to the right or to the left based on our situations. Life is uncertain, but our hope does not have to be uncertain too. Blessed are the people whose hope is planted in Christ Jesus because they know with certainty that God will give them victory in all situations. We can rely on God. He is the same every day. God will always be faithful even when we are unfaithful. God keeps His promises and He means what He says.

We are going to face many uncertain situations in our life and sometimes our hope will be the only thing that holds us together. Therefore, let us hang on to our hope and hang out with the one that we can have hope in. Keep hope alive! Amen! Praise God! Rejoice in the Lord Always!

DAY 274

"The Lord has established His throne in heaven, and His kingdom rules over all."
Psalm 103:19 NKJV

Let us make no mistake we are not in charge of nothing. The Lord is the only one qualified to be in charge in heaven and here on earth. The Lord is the Boss, President,

COO, Founder and Head Honcho over all. He has the final say in all situations. The Lord's "will" will be done and nobody can alter it. So let us patiently wait on the Lord's decision and not on man's decision.

And let us accept the Lord's decision, knowing that it is the best decision even if we do not agree or understand. The Lord loves us. He has our best interest at heart and He will only steer us in the right direction. The Lord cannot be voted or taken out of office. He is in charge for eternity. Amen! Praise God! Rejoice in the Lord Always!

DAY 275

"The people are strong and tall—Anakites! You know about them and have heard it said: "Who can stand up against the Anakites?" But be assured today that the Lord your God is the one who goes across ahead of you like a devouring fire. He will destroy them; he will subdue them before you."

Deuteronomy 9:2-3 NIV

Let us have no fear except for the fear of God. Let us rejoice and know we serve an awesome God who is greater and more powerful than anything or anyone we may encounter. Some things and some people

242

may appear to be mightier than God, but they are not. God can defeat them all.   So let us not worry or fear when we encounter problems or enemies bigger than us because we know the Lord is on our side.   Amen! Praise God! Rejoice in the Lord Always!

DAY 276

"The Spirit of the Lord will come upon you in power, and you will prophesy with them; and you will be changed into a different person."
1 Samuel 10:6 NIV

Once we accept Jesus Christ as our Lord and Savior, the Holy Spirit comes upon us and begins doing new and wonderful things in us. We get a second chance at life. We become anew again, with a whole new attitude.

We begin walking, talking and thinking in a completely new way. We change like a caterpillar changing into a beautiful butterfly. Not only are we changed from the inside to the outside, but also the things we are capable of doing are new.

We can fly like a butterfly when the Holy Spirit comes upon us and gives us the power to do things we have never been able to do before. Let us allow the Holy Spirit to come upon us. Amen! Praise God! Rejoice in the Lord Always!

DAY 277

"Now then, stand still and see this great thing the Lord is about to do before your eyes!"
1 Samuel 12:16 NIV

Sometimes we have to move out the way, stand still, and allow the Lord to work things out for us. When we have done all we can, let us stand still and wait upon the Lord. The Lord will work out everything for us according to His plan. We have to realize we can't solve every problem and we need the Lord's help. The Lord is here to help us even when everyone else has deserted us.

Let us not be our own worst enemy and miss our blessings by trying to do everything ourselves. Let us stand still, seek help from the Lord, and watch the great thing He will do before our eyes. Amen! Praise God! Rejoice in the Lord Always!

DAY 278

"This is the day the Lord has made; we will rejoice and be glad in it."
Psalm 118:24 NKJV

Many of us wake up each day and feel we have nothing to rejoice about, but we do.

Even in the midst of all of our challenges and obstacles, we have much to rejoice about. We have to look beyond our circumstances, our health, our finances and our loss, and look to God and thank Him for His many blessings.

Let us thank God for what we have and not cry about what we do not have. God did not bring us this far to leave us now. He has many more blessings waiting for us. So let us turn that frown upside down, rejoice, and thank God for a new day.

With every new day come new mercies. Hallelujah! We serve an awesome God and every day is a gift. If we concentrate on God instead of our circumstances, we will have plenty to rejoice about. Amen! Praise God! Rejoice in the Lord Always!

DAY 279

"But the angel answered and said to the women, "Do not be afraid, for I know that you seek Jesus who was crucified. He is not here; for He is risen, as He said."
Matthew 28:5-6a NKJV

Jesus is alive and well sitting at the right hand of the Father, interceding on our behalf. The tomb is empty. We no longer need to be afraid. Not even death can harm us now. The same power that raised Jesus from the grave is available to us. If we claim the power, we can have the victory over all of our troubles and live a life filled with faith, hope, joy and serenity.

Faith, hope, joy and serenity are essential elements we need to posses so that we can live the life God has planned for us. Jesus died on a Friday and rose on a Sunday so that we might have life and that we might have it abundantly. We are not afraid. We have the power! Amen! Praise God! Rejoice in the Lord Always!

DAY 280

"When He has tested me, I shall come forth as gold."

Job 23:10b NKJV

Many times, we are being tested by God as we go through our sufferings, hardships, trials and tribulations. God is testing the strength of our faith and commitment to Him. God wants to see what we do when trouble comes our way. God knows it is easy to have strong faith and commitment when life is good, but what do we do when times are not so good?

God wants to know: Do we trust Him? Does our faith waiver? Do we seek Him and pray? Do we depend on Him for guidance? Do we remember how He brought us through the last storm or do we curse Him?

Job says when he is tested; he shall come forth as gold. How will we come out? Will we pass the test? We will be blessed if we pass the test. Let our faith and commitment in the Lord be strong in and out of the storm. Go for the Gold! Amen! Praise God! Rejoice in the Lord Always!

DAY 281

"The Lord Almighty has sworn, "Surely, as I have planned, so it will be, and as I have purposed, so it will stand."
Isaiah 14:24 NIV

There is a reason for everything that happens in our life and it is all geared towards God fulfilling His plan and purpose. So no matter what difficulties or crisis comes our way, let us stand strong and never give up. It just may be all a part of God's plan.

God's plan calls for us to achieve great and wonderful things and sometimes He uses our crisis to get our attention and put us on the right path. God's great plan for our life can only be carried out if we just hold on and trust Him.

Sometimes we have to go through something to get to the place God wants us to be. Let us hold on, trust God, and know the best is yet to come and trouble does not last forever. Amen! Praise God! Rejoice in the Lord Always!

DAY 282

"Set your minds on things above, not on earthly things."

Colossians 3:2 NIV

Let us choose to wake up each morning with our minds stayed on thee. Let us say "Good Morning Lord." The Lord brings many blessings and goodness into our life and it is good to remind ourselves of that each morning. When we set our minds on Christ, we begin to view life as He sees it and we set our priorities from it.

We will wake up with sunshine in our hearts even on cloudy days knowing God has a purpose for our living. It will make it easier to get up and put our feet on the ground. It will be more difficult to be scared of failure and harder to waller in self-pity and despair.

The Lord gives us power and strength to meet our daily challenges and hope for the future. Let us keep our mind on things that are eternal and not temporary. For the things of the world are temporary and they fade away, but things of God are eternal and last for eternity. Amen! Praise God! Rejoice in the Lord Always!

DAY 283

"But you, when you pray, go into your room, and when you have shut your door, pray to your Father who is in the secret place; and your Father who sees in secret will reward you openly."

Matthew 6:6 NKJV

Sometimes God wants some quiet time with us. He wants to talk to us alone with no audience or interruptions because what He has to say is meant for us only. Noise and others will only keep us from concentrating on God and we will miss what He has to say.

Prayer time is important. It is our private communion with God and our time to evoke God into our presence and communicate with Him. So let us steal away to that quiet place where we will find only God. Amen! Praise God! Rejoice in the Lord Always!

DAY 284

"Submit to God and be at peace with Him; in this way prosperity will come to you."
                                        Job 22:21 NIV

If we are tired of failure, not living life to its fullest or we want something more out of life, let us try submitting ourselves to God. God will give us a life worth rejoicing and celebrating. We will have a new life filled with success and prosperity.

God will take us to new heights and places we have never even thought about going. God will strengthen us and we will do things we thought were once impossible. We will encounter the same old problems, crises and circumstances, but we will not see or handle them the same way as before. We will be victorious over them instead of them being victorious over us.

"Submitting to God" means giving ourselves totally to Him and following in all His ways. When we see the results, we will be glad we did. God is Great all of the time! Amen! Praise God! Rejoice in the Lord Always!

DAY 285

"Then King David went in and sat before the Lord; and he said: "Who am I, O Lord God? And what is my house, that You have brought me this far?"

1 Chronicles 17:16 NKJV

Let us count our blessings one by one. We have come a mighty long way on the many blessings the Lord has bestowed upon us. The Lord has blessed us not because of who we are, but because of His love, grace and mercy. We can't earn and we don't deserve many of the blessings we have received, but the Lord has blessed us anyhow. The Lord is so good to us. He loves us and He wants us to be at peace, be joyful, and be able to celebrate the life He has planned for us.

The Lord has brought us a mighty long way and He is not done with us yet. He has many more blessings to give us. Let us thank the Lord for what He has done for us because He didn't have to do it, but He did. Thank you Lord for there is none like you! Amen! Praise God! Rejoice in the Lord Always!

DAY 286

"The LORD is my rock and my fortress and my deliverer; My God, my strength, in whom I will trust;"

Psalm 18:2 NKJV

The Lord is many things to us. He is our everything. Whatever we need the Lord to be at that moment, He is. In the midst of our troubles, the Lord is our rock, fortress and deliverer. He will protect and deliver us from anyone or anything that is causing us trouble, harm, sorrow, loss or hardship. The Lord mighty and powerful is our rock. He can't be moved by anyone or anything that we might encounter.

As our fortress, the Lord is our place of safety where we can run and find protection and peace. We can find strength from the Lord to endure just by reminding ourselves that He is there for us and He is everything we need. Let us trust in the Lord! Amen! Praise God! Rejoice in the Lord Always!

DAY 287

"The Lord is with me; he is my helper."
Psalm 118:7 NIV

The Lord is willing and able to help us in our time of need. He is the helper to the helpless. In order for the Lord to help us, we first must admit that we need help. Let us call on the Lord and let Him know we need His help now and always. We can't do it alone. We can accomplish a lot more, do more good, and be more successful in life with the Lord's help.

Many of us are too proud to ask for help and we struggle unnecessarily. It does not mean we are a failure because we need and ask for help. It is alright to ask for help from the Lord. He wants to help and He does not want His children to struggle. It is the wise who realize they need help and asks for it.

The Lord is there to help us and overcome anything that tries to hold us back. Wherever and whenever we need help, the Lord is there. Call on Him! Amen! Praise God! Rejoice in the Lord Always!

DAY 288

"Command those who are rich in this present world not to be arrogant nor to put their hope in wealth, which is so uncertain, but to put their hope in God, who richly provides us with everything for our enjoyment."
1 Timothy 6:17 NIV

Let us not live with a false sense of security which money can provide. Many of us believe that money is the key to happiness and depend on it to provide for all of our needs. And when the money does not come in, because of loss of work or health, or if it gets lost in business or stock market, we fall apart with depression and despair.

We can't put our hope in things that are not certain and depend on them to provide for us. We can put our hope in God for only He is always certain. God never changes. We can be certain that God will always provide for us. He is our Jehovah Jireh (which means God is our provider), not money. God will provide the money when we need it. Let us seek God first. He is priceless. Amen! Praise God! Rejoice in the Lord Always!

DAY 289

"Blessed is he whose transgression is forgiven, whose sin is covered."
Psalm 32:1 NKJV

We all have said or done things that we are truly sorry for later. We are not perfect and God knows that. That is why He will forgive us for the wrong we do and remember it no more. We serve a God who is compassionate and loving. He wants to forgive us and bring us back in a right relationship with Him. God does not want His children to walk around in the pain that being sorry can bring.

Therefore, let us go before the Lord, admit what we did, and say how sorry we are. Then we can celebrate in the joy of His forgiveness. God is good all the time. Let us thank God for His grace and mercy. Amen! Praise God! Rejoice in the Lord Always!

DAY 290

"But take notice, the hour is coming, and it has arrived, when you will all be dispersed and scattered, every man to his own home, leaving me alone. Yet I am not alone, because the Father is with me."
John 16:32 AMP

We might think we are alone when no one else is around, but we are not. Let us be encouraged and know that God is always with us. God will follow us around day and night. He is everywhere we are. When we allow God into our life, He never leaves. We may not have human contact, but we have God and He is better than the rest.

So when we want someone to talk with, let us talk with God. He is always available and never too busy to listen to what we have to say. He will comfort us in time of sorrow and joy, and carry us during our darkest times. God is the best company we can keep. He is our all in all. Amen! Praise God! Rejoice in the Lord Always!

DAY 291

"Remain in me, and I will remain in you. No branch can bear fruit by itself; it must remain in the vine. Neither can you bear fruit unless you remain in me."

John 15:4 NIV

Just as a tree needs water, we need Jesus. Water is nourishment for the tree. It helps the tree to grow and flourish. Jesus is our nourishment. He is our Bread of Life. He nourishes and gives life to our body, soul and spirit so we too can grow and flourish. Jesus

256

nourishes us through prayer, meditation, His Word, and through use of others.

When we are nourished by Jesus, we become strong and have the strength to withstand any storm. Let us seek Jesus with our heart, soul and mind so we can be fed our "Daily Bread." Let us not begin our day without first being fed. Did you receive your nourishment today? Amen! Praise God! Rejoice in the Lord Always!

DAY 292

"For God has not given us a spirit of fear, but of power and of love and of a sound mind."
                    2 Timothy 1:7 NKJV

Yes, we can! We can do it. Whatever we want to do, we can do it even the impossible. We are more than conquerors because we have the power of God in us. God blesses us with His supernatural power so we can do extraordinary things. So the next time something comes along and it is bigger than us, let us remember we have the power.

Let us claim our power so we can claim our victory, success, and future. God did not instill in us to be fearful and timid, so let us not claim them. When we say we can't, we are telling God He can't. With God everything and anything is possible. Amen! Praise God! Rejoice in the Lord Always!

DAY 293

"It happened after this that David inquired of the Lord, saying, "Shall I go up to any of the cities of Judah?" And the Lord said to him, "Go up." David said, "Where shall I go up?" And He said, "To Hebron."
2 Samuel 2:1 NKJV

Before David made a move, he took the matter to the Lord so that he would make the right move at the right time. David wanted the Lord's will to be done in his life and not his own. Let us also go to the Lord to seek guidance and direction for our life. The Lord is the Master Planner. He has the blueprint for our life. He knows what, when and where we should do, say and go.

If we never ask the Lord what, when and where, we may never know what He has planned for us. The moves we make on our own could be right or wrong, but the moves the Lord tells us to make are always right. God is all-knowing, so let us seek His advice first. Amen! Praise God! Rejoice in the Lord Always!

DAY 294

"But this I say: He who sows sparingly will also reap sparingly, and he who sows bountiful will reap bountifully."
2 Corinthians 9:6 NKJV

It is more important how we give than how much we give. We can give a little if we are giving from the heart, not looking for anything in return. If we give all we can, trusting God will supply all we need. We won't get something for nothing, so we have to give if we want to receive. God has blessed us with many things to share and to give to others.

We have our time, love, skills, money, talent and knowledge. And anytime we don't know what or how much to give or share let us pray to God and allow Him to lead our heart. God did not bless us with these things to hold or to horde, but to use them to be a blessing to others. Amen! Praise God! Rejoice in the Lord Always!

DAY 295

"After this, Jesus went out and saw a tax collector by the name of Levi sitting at his tax booth, "Follow me," Jesus said to him, and Levi got up, left everything and followed Him."

Luke 5:27-28 NIV

When Jesus calls us, we have to be willing to give up our material fortune for a spiritual fortune. We have to be willing to lose all we have gained in order to gain what Jesus has for us. If we are not willing to let go of the old, we can't take hold of the new that Jesus has waiting for us.

Jesus has something great for us to do and we never thought about doing it for ourselves. He will take the ordinary and make them extraordinary. Jesus' ways and thoughts are not our ways and thoughts. His are much higher. Let us go when Jesus calls. We can't beat His giving no matter how hard we try. Amen! Praise God! Rejoice in the Lord Always!

DAY 296

"This is my commandment, that you love one another as I have loved you."

John 15:12 NKJV

God first loved us. Yet when we were sinners, God gave us His only begotten Son. God calls us to love all humanity and not hate or discriminate. We are all His children and we all deserve love and respect. True love prevails when we love people who don't love us. It is harder to love someone when they don't love us. We can show love to others by helping, giving, encouraging, smiling, and listening.

A little love goes a long way. We are to look past peoples' faults and love them anyway. We can hate their action and love them as a person. We all have faults and yet we want to be loved. The more love we give, the more love we receive. God is love! Make someone's day and show him some love. Amen! Praise God! Rejoice in the Lord Always!

DAY 297

"I guide you in the way of wisdom and lead you along straight paths. When you walk, your steps will not be hampered; when you run, you will not stumble."

Proverbs 4:11-12 NIV

Let us not be wise in our own eyes, but seek true wisdom that comes from the Lord. Godly wisdom teaches, guides and trains us in the way we should go so we can have a life rich with many blessings. Living in this world with temptation all around us, we need Godly wisdom to give us direction, help us set boundaries, and to help us stay on the right path. When we seek true wisdom from God, we find many benefits including wealth, peace, long life, success and honor.

Finding Godly wisdom is more valuable than finding silver or gold. True wisdom does not come from our friends or us, it comes from the Lord. Amen! Praise God! Rejoice in the Lord Always!

DAY 298

"But blessed are your eyes because they see, and your ears because they hear."
                                        Matthew 13:16 NIV

Let us open our eyes so we can see and open our ears so we can hear the wonderful things the Lord has done for our family, friends, loved ones and us. When we see and hear what the Lord has done, we can begin to believe and have faith in Him.

We will know without a doubt that no matter what difficulties we face, we will survive because the Lord gives us strength to climb every mountain, swim every ocean, and jump every hurdle. We will know that even if our problems are not settled today or tomorrow, we should hold on and never give up.

We know that with God, there is a light at the end of the tunnel, a pot of gold at the end of the rainbow, and joy comes in the morning. Let us go and tell what the Lord has done for us and through us, so other people can see and hear about the goodness of the Lord. The Lord has been so good to us! Amen! Praise God! Rejoice in the Lord Always!

DAY 299

"Come with me by yourselves to a quiet place and get some rest."
Mark 6:31b NIV

We hustle and bustle day in and day out with so much on our mind that we rarely ever get our proper rest. We might lie down to sleep, but we don't get any rest because we keep so much stuff on our mind. When we don't take care of ourselves and get the rest we need, we become weak and vulnerable to many of the devil's schemes. The devil likes to attack our mind when we are tired and weak because he knows it is hard for us to think rational at those times.

We can't get our proper rest until we give all that stuff that is weighing us down to the Lord in prayer. So let us steal away to a quiet place where we can only find Jesus and allow Him to give us rest and renew our body, soul, and spirit. Let Go, Let God! Amen! Praise God! Rejoice in the Lord Always!

DAY 300

"Don't be deceived, my dear brothers. Every good and perfect gift is from above, coming down from the father of the heavenly lights, who does not change like shifting shadows."
                                   James 1:16-17 NIV

When good things happen to us, many of us believe it is because we have been "lucky." But "luck" has nothing to do with our receiving anything good. Things that happen to us are never by luck because God has already planned all of our steps. Every good and perfect gift that we receive is a blessing from God. We rob God of His glory when we fail to see the good we receive as blessings from above.

So let us not expect anything to happen when we cross our fingers and wish for "good luck," but let us expect something to happen when we get on our knees and pray. There is power in prayer. Luck has never given us anything. It is God who gives. Amen! Praise God! Rejoice in the Lord Always!

DAY 301

"Those who trust in the Lord are like Mount Zion, which cannot be shaken but endures forever."

Psalm 125:1 NIV

When we trust in the Lord, we learn how to look at life and live life in a brand new way. No longer are we falling apart and ready to give up when trouble comes our way. We learn how to stand strong through all kinds of storms. We learn we have nothing to fear because the Lord will always be there.

We learn we could have joy and peace in the midst of the storm. We learn how to find faith and hope in the Lord. We learn the Lord will always provide and He is always on time. We learn failure is not an option, but success is. We learn how to hold on and wait on the Lord. With the Lord, we will always endure. Trust Him! Amen! Praise God! Rejoice in the Lord Always!

DAY 302

"I have come into the world as a light, so that no one who believes in me should stay in darkness."

John 12:46 NIV

Who or what shall inspire us? Let us allow God and His Word to be the source of our inspiration so He can brighten up our darkest days. We can be inspired just by knowing God keeps His promises. He will do what He said He would do and by knowing God, He will do for us as He has done for others.

God and His Word are true and powerful. They will lift us up, turn us around, and put our feet on solid ground. We will have joy in our heart and a new song to sing; a reason and a purpose to get up, persevere, and live life.

God has come into this world to be our light in the midst of our darkness and His light shall never go out. Amen! Praise God! Rejoice in the Lord Always!

DAY 303

"If you do not stand firm in your faith, you will not stand at all."

Isaiah 7:9b NIV

We will not be able to succeed or achieve if we really don't believe. Let us stand firm and hold on to the faith we profess no matter what happens. Let us not allow anything or anyone to rob us of our faith.

God is real, He has something waiting for all of us, and He will deliver it in His time not ours. However, if we really don't believe it, we will not receive it. If we truly believe, we will claim it, put our faith into action, and speak into existence what God has for us before we see it.

So let us put our fear to the side, pick up our faith and go after what God has for us. Because we claim to have faith, we have to put our faith into action. James 2:26 tells us "For as the body without the spirit is dead, so faith without works is dead also." God is real. Keep the Faith! Amen! Praise God! Rejoice in the Lord Always!

DAY 304

"I desire to do your will, O my God; your law is within my heart."

Psalm 40:8 NIV

Life gets better and brighter when we choose to allow God's will to be done in our life instead of our own. God can do for us

what we can't do for ourselves. And sometimes God will derail the plans we have set for
our life so His "will" will be done.

So when we make plans for that career or
that house or that school and they get
derailed let us not cry, holler or scream, but
rejoice and know God's will is being done.
And His "will" is much better than ours.

So let us not fight against God's will, but
humbly submit to it so we can live that better
life. Let us pray to God and tell Him we
desire His will to be done. God knows what's
best for us even when we don't. Amen!
Praise God! Rejoice in the Lord Always.

DAY 305

*"For the day of trouble he will keep me safe in
his dwellings; he will hide me in the shelter of
his tabernacle and set me high upon a rock."*
Psalm 27:5 NIV

Let us find peace and joy in the midst of
our troubles by knowing God will keep us
safe. He will set us far above all of our
troubles where they cannot cause us any pain
or sorrow. We will be able to turn our grief
into joy knowing our troubles can't harm us
no more. When we trust in the Lord and put

our hope in Him, He makes all of our troubles work out for our good.

God can do all things except fail so He can turn any situation around. Even when it seems like nothing is working out, let us know the Lord is working everything out and our blessing is coming. Let us find the Lord in our times of trouble so we can find peace and joy. Amen! Praise God! Rejoice in the Lord Always!

DAY 306

"So David went on and became great, and the Lord God of hosts was with him."
2 Samuel 5:10 NKJV

We are destined for greatness when we are obedient and follow in the ways of the Lord. God pours out many blessings upon us, uses us in a mighty way, and we become much greater than we ever conceived for ourselves. With God, there is nothing we cannot do or overcome. We see and live life in a different way and it becomes worth rejoicing and celebrating.

When we follow God, He does not expect us to be perfect but He does expect us to strive to become perfect. Let us keep our eye on the prize, which is Christ Jesus. The Lord knows the way to greatness and when we follow Him, He shows us the way and we are guaranteed to get there. Let us grab hold of what the Lord has for us. Amen! Praise God! Rejoice in the Lord Always!

DAY 307

"Even to your old age and gray hairs I am he, I am he who will sustain you."
                                    Isaiah 46:4 NIV

Our dreams can come true. We can make it through all of our trials and tribulations and we can succeed because we serve a Great God who sustains us from everlasting to everlasting. God is Mighty and Powerful. He sustains us with His power, strength, love, guidance, grace and mercy. God will sustain us even in our darkest hour so let us not allow others to deter us from succeeding with their negativity.

Some people might say we can't make it, give up or we might not amount to nothing, but let us remember it is to God whom we must listen. God has the last and final word, not man. So let us keep hope alive and keep persevering despite what others might think or say. It is God. It is He who is with us and sustains us from birth to eternity. Amen! Praise God! Rejoice in the Lord Always!

DAY 308

"The grace of our Lord Jesus Christ be with you."
1 Corinthians 16:23 NKJV

Let us be encouraged and know God's grace is upon us every day as we go about our daily life. Let us look around and see "if it had not been for the grace of God." We might not have all we want, but we have all we need. We might have done some things wrong, but we have another chance to get them right. We might be facing hardship today, but trouble does not last forever. We might not know where our next meal is coming from, but we know we will be fed.

God pours His grace upon us not because we are so good, but because He loves us that much. Let us have faith and hope in our Lord Jesus Christ because it is by His grace that we will make it through. It is by the grace of God! Thank Him! Amen! Praise God! Rejoice in the Lord Always!

DAY 309

"But, "Let him who boasts boast in the Lord."
2 Corinthians 10:17 NIV

Let us give God the glory and praise that is due Him. God deserves the highest praise "Hallelujah" from us at all times. For it is He who makes everything possible and not we ourselves. God has done many great things for us and through us. When we succeed or accomplish anything, it is because God made it happen. God is the one that opens the doors, put people and things in our life to help, and the one who makes a way out of no way.

So when we boast, let us boast in the Lord. Let us tell others how God has blessed us and made it all possible. Let us boast about His greatness so others will come to know Him too. God gets all the glory and praise! When praises go up, blessings come down. Amen! Praise God! Rejoice in the Lord Always!

DAY 310

"Oh come, let us sing to the Lord! Let us shout joyfully to the Rock of our salvation. Let us come before His presence with thanksgiving; Let us shout joyfully to Him with psalms."

Psalm 95:1-2 NKJV

We can never thank the Lord enough for all the blessings He bestows upon us morning,

272

noon and night. The Lord is so good to us. He takes care of us better than we do ourselves. He gives us what we need before we even know we need it. The Lord has done so much for us already and He is not finished yet.

So with an attitude of gratitude and a grateful heart, let us kneel before the Lord's throne of grace and say "Thank you, thank you Lord." When we think about all the Lord has done, we can't help but to shout, scream, yell or cry "Thank you." The Lord is worthy to be praised! Amen! Praise God! Rejoice in the Lord Always

DAY 311

"Furthermore King David said to all assembly: "My son Solomon, whom alone God has chosen, is young and inexperienced; and the work is great, because the temple is not for man but for the Lord God."
1 Chronicles 29:1 NKJV

Let us know when the Lord chooses us for a great task -- doing something we have never done nor have the skills to do. He will be with us and give us the skills and resources we need to get the task done. Whatever the Lord calls us to do, He will see us through. So let us step out on faith, be strong, and do it.

With the Lord by our side, we can't fail because He can do everything but fail. We lead our own selves down the road to failure when we carry those negative thoughts such as "I can't" or "I am not qualified." The Lord knows we can when He chooses us. God sees the best in us. The work we do is for the Lord, not man. Amen! Praise God! Rejoice in the Lord Always!

DAY 312

"Nothing in all creation is hidden from God's sight."

Hebrews 4:13 NIV

We might not see and know everything that is going on, but God does. Everything and everyone is in God's presence always. He is an all-knowing God. God knows everything before it happens and He knows how everything will end. That is why it is important for us to seek God for answers, guidance, and direction. For only God can tell us about the present and the future, not horoscopes or fortunetellers.

The next time we face any trouble of any kind, let us remember that God knows all about our situation and He has already taken care of it so there is no need for us to worry. Let us trust and follow God because He can see what we are unable to see. Amen! Praise God! Rejoice in the Lord Always!

DAY 313

"The word of the Lord you have spoken is good," Hezekiah replied."
Isaiah 39:8 NIV

What we say sometimes is not always good and pleasing to the Lord or to the person to whom we are speaking. Let us be slow to speak and think about how our words will affect someone before we speak them. Let us allow our words to build up, encourage, show love, and comfort others.

We are all going through something and a kind word can make a difference. The words we speak are determined by what is in our heart. If jealously is in our heart, then our words will reflect the jealously. If love is in our heart, then our words will reflect the love.

Let us keep our mind on the Lord so the words we speak can come from the Lord. Let us pray daily to the Lord and recite scripture. Psalm 19:14 says "Let the words of my mouth and the meditation of my heart be acceptable in your sight, O Lord, my Rock and my

Redeemer." Amen! Praise God! Rejoice in the Lord Always!

DAY 314

"Only be careful, and watch yourselves closely so that you do not forget the things your eyes have seen or let them slip from your heart as long as you live.

Deuteronomy 4:9 NIV

When things in our life are going bad we scream, holler and cry out to the Lord for help, but as soon as He helps and the good times come, we forget many times what the Lord has done. But, it is important for us to remember what the Lord has done for us because when trouble arises again that memory about what the Lord has done now becomes our Spiritual Energy.

Spiritual Energy is released when we remember, and it gives us the power and strength to persevere and endure despite what is going on in our life because we know from memory that the Lord will rescue, save and deliver us just as He did before. Trouble can no longer rob us of our joy! Let us remember and not forget the great and many things the Lord has done. Amen! Praise God! Rejoice in the Lord Always!

DAY 315

"Give heed to the voice of my cry, my King and my God, for to you I will pray."
                    Psalm 5:2 NKJV

Prayer is powerful! When we pray to God, it makes all weapons formed against us weak and it makes us strong. The enemy knows how much power there is in prayer and he does everything in his power to stop us from praying. He knows God can extinguish all flaming arrows in our life so they cannot harm us no more.

The enemy tries to stop us from praying by telling us we are too busy, we don't have time, we don't know how to pray, God does not hear us, or nothing is going to change.

Let us remember whatever the enemy tells us is a lie. Prayer helps us to keep our relationship with God strong, it helps us to keep God in our presence, and it lets God know we depend on Him. Let us pray every day and keep the enemy weak! Amen! Praise God! Rejoice in the Lord Always!

DAY 316

"Be still, and know that I am God;"
                    Psalm 46:10 NKJV

Sometimes we can be too busy; so busy that it distracts us from what is really important in our life. In Luke 10:38-42, Martha is busy cleaning and preparing the house and she complains to Jesus that her sister Mary is not helping her. Instead, Mary has chosen to be still and listen to Jesus. Jesus tells Martha that Mary has chosen what is better.

Let us be like Mary and choose not to be too busy, but choose to take time out and be still so we can listen to Jesus. In our stillness, we have time to pray, meditate on the Word of God, listen to His small voice speaking to us, reflect on His goodness, and know that He is God.

Listening to Jesus feeds and gives strength to our spirit. Lord, teach us how to "Be still" and listen to you. Amen! Praise God! Rejoice in the Lord Always!

DAY 317

"Get wisdom! Get understanding! Do not forget, nor turn away from the words of my mouth. Do not forsake her, and she will preserve you; love her, and she will keep you."

Proverbs 4:5-6 NKJV

278

Let us allow wisdom and understanding to be our best friends. Let us cherish and search for them daily in the Word of God where true wisdom and understanding can be found. True wisdom and understanding comes from God; trusting Him and applying His Word to our daily life.

Wisdom and understanding will keep us and lead us in the right direction so we can rejoice and celebrate life. Let us trust God and store His Word in our heart because "No one is wiser and more knowledgeable than God. No, not one." Amen! Praise God! Rejoice in the Lord Always!

DAY 318

"So Pharaoh said to Joseph, "I hereby put you in charge of the whole land of Egypt."
Genesis 41:41 NIV

In everybody's life some rain will fall, but we can dance in the rain if we keep our faith and trust in the Lord. Through it all, He will not let us slip or fall. Just when we think we are about to slip or fall, the Lord will lift us up and take our feet off shaky ground.

Joseph encountered many storms just as many of us will and the Lord never let him slip or fall. In his life, Joseph was sold by his brothers, separated from his family, put in prison, and was falsely accused. And through it all, Joseph kept praising, hoping, and trusting in the Lord. Joseph knew the Lord was faithful and He would bring him through.

In the end, for hanging on through it all, Joseph received his blessing. If we hang on through it all, we will receive our blessing. So let us dance in the rain and hang on through it all. Amen! Praise God! Rejoice in the Lord Always!

DAY 319

"He gives power to the weak, and to those who have no might He increases strength."
                                Isaiah 40:29 NKJV

Sometimes life drains us of all the strength and energy we have, but all is not hopeless because we serve a good God who is always there and on time when we need Him. When we are weak and we call on God, by His grace He bestows upon us His power and increases our strength with His strength so we are no longer weak. Hallelujah!

Life might sometimes press us hard on every side; but thanks be to God, we are not crushed. With God by our side, we will "mount up with wings like eagles," soar above all of our hardships, crisis and storms, and never grow weary. God is our source of power and strength. Let us stay plugged in. Amen! Praise God! Rejoice in the Lord Always!

DAY 320

"Devote yourselves to prayer, being watchful and thankful."
                                    Colossians 4:2 NIV

If we want things in our life to change for the better, let us pray. Let us pray continually knowing that our Father in heaven hears our prayers and that He will answer them in His time. Prayer is our conversation with God when we not only pray for ourselves, but also for our love ones, enemies, family and friends.

It is also a time when we go humbly before the Lord in a child-like manner and confess our sins; seek His guidance, and direction for our life. We must show God some admiration by telling Him how great and wonderful He is. And prayer is a time when we thank the Lord for all of His many blessings and goodness. God is listening, so let us pray. Amen! Praise God! Rejoice in the Lord Always!

DAY 321

"Therefore, whether you eat or drink, or whatever you do, do all to the glory of God."
1 Corinthians 10:31 NKJV

Let us be mindful of the things we do and how we do them. Let us not look to glorify man or ourselves, but let us look to glorify God. Let us exalt the "name of Jesus" in everything we do.

God is so good to us. He is the one that blesses us and makes everything possible. So let us please Him with our actions and deeds. Let us show God how much we love and appreciate Him. Let us allow others to see the "Jesus" in us, for we are ambassadors for Christ.

God knows we will never be perfect. He just wants us to do things for the right reason and to the best of our God-given ability. Let us call on the Holy Spirit to lead and guide us so we will operate according to God's will and not man. Glorify God and not the world. Amen! Praise God! Rejoice in the Lord Always!

DAY 322

"Above all be sure you take faith as your shield, for it can quench every burning missile the enemy hurls at you."
Ephesians 6:16 NIV

Our purpose in life is to do God's will and sometimes we may feel that we are unqualified to fulfill the task. Let us have faith and know that God will supply us with everything we need to accomplish the goal. The enemy (Satan) will try to prevent us from completing our goals by putting doubt and obstacles in our path.

The enemy will attack our family members, our health, financial situation, and our relationship with God. Don't be discouraged; keep praising God for the good and bad. It only reassures us that we must be doing something good and growing to our next spiritual level in the Lord. Be of good courage. Have faith that if God said it, He will do it! This too shall pass! Amen! Praise God! Rejoice in the Lord Always!

Written by Delorise Reuben-McDuffie

DAY 323

"But thanks be to God! He gives us the victory through our Lord Jesus Christ."

1 Corinthians 15:57 NIV

Jesus Christ achieved the ultimate victory when He defeated death on the cross. And when we keep our feet anchored in Jesus, we can stand firm until the victory is won in all of our struggles. It is not "if we will have the victory," it is "we will have the victory." There is nothing too hard for God! He gives us the victory through Jesus Christ. Hallelujah!

So in all of our circumstances, let us find faith, hope and serenity because the battle has already been won. The victory is ours, thanks be to God! Let us graciously accept God's invitation to come into His presence so we too can receive the victory through Jesus Christ. Amen! Praise God! Rejoice in the Lord Always!

DAY 324

"Be joyful in hope, patient in affliction, faithful in prayer."

Romans 12:12 NIV

284

No one likes to suffer and suffering is not easy, but it is inevitable that we all will suffer sometime in our life. And if we hold on to the promises of the Lord faithful in prayer, we can be joyful in hope and patient in affliction.

We can come out of our affliction a stronger and better person with a closer relationship with God, more endurance, hope and perseverance.

Facing affliction without God's spiritual strength can lead to unnecessary stress, depression, and despair. God is here for us so why face affliction without Him. Call on the Lord and let us be joyful in hope and patient in affliction. Amen! Praise God! Rejoice in the Lord Always!

DAY 325

"They are brought to their knees and fall, but we rise up and stand firm."
Psalm 20:8 NIV

Some people fall and never get up, but we rise and stand firm because we put our hope and trust in the Lord. With the Lord by our side, we can rise and stand firm against anything, any person, and any crisis.

We know nothing can prosper against us because the Lord is greater than any problem we may face. The Lord is strong and mighty. He has our back. He upholds us with His right hand and He never lets us fall.

David rose and stood firm against Goliath the giant because He trusted in the Lord. David knew the Lord would work everything out for his good. And the Lord did. He gave David the victory over Goliath the giant.

We can trust the Lord to be there with us every step of the way and give us the victory so let us rise and stand firm against the giants in our life. No need to fall. Let us rise and stand firm! Amen! Praise God! Rejoice in the Lord Always!

DAY 326

"Seek the Lord while He may be found, call upon Him while He is near."
Isaiah 55:6 NKJV

"Why should we put off until tomorrow what we can do today?" For tomorrow is not promised to any of us. Let us put all other business aside and put God first. Let us make seeking the Lord with all our heart and soul top priority in our life today. Let us call on the Lord with a willing heart and receive the many blessings He has waiting for us.

The Lord has come into our life so that we may have life and have it more abundantly. But we have to seek Him in order to receive it. Don't we all want a better life filled with blessings, faith, hope, joy and serenity? Don't we all want to rejoice and celebrate life? God is knocking, let us open the door and let Him in today! Amen! Praise God! Rejoice in the Lord Always!

DAY 327

"Jesus said to him, "Thomas, because you have seen Me, you have believed. Blessed are those who have not seen and yet have believed."

John 20:29 NKJV

We might not be able to see Jesus with our eyes but we all have seen and can testify to what He can do, and what He will do for others and us. We can feel and hear Jesus with our heart, body, soul, and spirit.

Jesus is real without a doubt. The Word of God has been written for our benefit so that we might believe through the testimonies of others, by His miracles, healings, blessings and wonderful deeds.

When we believe in Jesus, we can let go and let God. We can trust and have faith in

Him to lead us even when we can't see where we are going. We can allow Him to be the Author of our life story, knowing it is going to have a happy ending. Let us tell the world "Jesus Christ was born." Let us believe! Amen! Praise God! Rejoice in the Lord Always!

DAY 328

"Though I walk in the midst of trouble you preserve my life"

Psalm 138:7 NIV

Let us know whatever difficulties life throws at us, God will see us through them. God will be with us to keep us and protect us from the negative effects trouble brings. With God, trouble has no power over us because God does not give us more than we can handle. We are stronger than we think. We have the strength of God within us and we will make it through.

Let us know that there is a light at the end of the tunnel and our troubles won't last forever because God promises to deliver us from all of our troubles. God will work out all of our troubles according to His will and in His time. Let us hold on to God's unchanging hands and never let go. Amen! Praise God! Rejoice in the Lord Always!

288

DAY 329

"Let us come before His presence with thanksgiving; let us shout joyfully to Him with psalms."

Psalm 95:2 NKJV

Let us humbly come before the Lord and Praise His Holy Name. All Glory and honor belongs to the Lord our Maker, the creator of the heavens and earth. He is so good to us. He is worthy to be praised. Let us bow down before God with thanksgiving in our heart and thank Him for all He has done. For it is God who makes the impossible possible. He is the one who keeps us from falling day after day. He is the one who picked us up and turned our life around.

It was not our neighbor, spouse or child. It was God. Let us thank Him! We might not realize it but sometimes we have much to be thankful for! Let us count our blessings, one by one. Amen! Praise God! Rejoice in the Lord Always!

DAY 330

"For our light and momentary troubles are achieving for us an eternal glory that far outweighs them all."

2 Corinthians 4:17 NIV

We might not like having troubles, but they are good for something. Yes, our suffering serves a purpose and God has made it so that something good can come out of suffering. Jesus Christ's suffering served a purpose and we have everlasting life because of it. So the benefits we get and the lessons we learn from our troubles outweigh the suffering we might have to go through.

Suffering is not easy and sometimes we want to give up, but don't! Call on God instead. He is here with us to give us strength when we are weak so we can endure and persevere through the storm. Let us not miss our lesson or our blessing! Let us keep the faith and stay the course! Amen! Praise God! Rejoice in the Lord Always!

DAY 331

"All the days ordained for me were written in your book before one of them came to be."
Psalm 139:16 NIV

Our destiny has already been planned out for us before we were formed in our mother's womb. God has ordained our life and every step we take with success and prosperity. If we just let go of the plans we made for ourselves, we can then walk into the plans God has ordained for us. God's plans for us are bigger and better than we can ever imagine.

So let us stop crying and weeping but rejoice when our plans do not work out because the best is yet to come. We might come face to face with some trial and tribulations along the way, but don't let us put a period where God has put a comma. Our plans may be good but God's plans are better. Amen! Praise God! Rejoice in the Lord Amen!

DAY 332

"But we have this treasure in earthen vessels, that the excellence of the power may be of God and not us."
2 Corinthians 4:7 NKJV

Jesus Christ died on a Friday and rose on a Sunday with all power in His hand. And that same power Jesus rose with lies within us for us to use when our natural power just is not enough. Our natural power has its limits to which it can achieve and conquer but God's Spiritual Power is unlimited. "We can do all things through Christ which strengths us."

So it is through the power of God in which we achieve and conquer our goals. When we don't use our spiritual power instilled in us by Jesus Christ, it becomes easy for the enemy's power to penetrate our heart, soul and spirit. This then causes us to fail, give-up, and feel depressed.

There is no greater power than the power of God. Let us plug into Jesus for our source of power. Amen! Praise God! Rejoice in the Lord Always!

DAY 333

"Do you not know that your body is a temple of the Holy Spirit, who is in you, whom you have received from God? You are not your own: you were bought at a price. Therefore honor God with your body."
1 Corinthians 6:19-20 NIV

Let us be mindful of how we act, what we say, and what we wear because our body is a temple that houses God's Holy Spirit. Jesus Christ paid the price so we can have the benefit of the Holy Spirit residing in us. So when we talk right, walk right, and do right, we are showing God that we know how to love the Holy Spirit.

The Holy Spirit teaches, guides, helps, comforts, and counsels us so that we don't have to be alone or face anything alone. Our body is a priceless temple so let us take care of the house in which the Holy Spirit resides. Amen! Praise God! Rejoice in the Lord Always!

DAY 334

"When they had seen him, they spread the word concerning what had been told them about this child, and all who heard it were amazed at what the shepherds said to them."
Luke 2:17-18 NIV

For a Child is born in a manger. He came to save us from the sins of the world. So we could have a second chance to get it right and live a life full of blessings, success and prosperity. He shall be called "Prince of Peace, "Wonderful," "Counselor," "Everlasting Father," and "Mighty God." Let us too spread the word that a "Child has been born."

The world will know about the goodness of the Lord and they too can be saved and live a life full of faith, hope and serenity. "Every knee shall bow and every tongue shall confess that Jesus Christ is Lord." Amen!

DAY 335

"O God, do not keep silent; be not quiet, O God, be not still."
Psalm 83:1 NIV

When we don't see God move or hear Him speak when we think we should, we feel God has forgotten all about our troubles and us. But let us know God is always faithful to us. He will never leave nor forsake us. When God is silent, let us just stand firm, be patient, have faith, and wait for Him to see us through.

He will answer us and work everything out according to His will and purpose. God moves according to His time and not ours. He knows the best time to execute the plan! We don't know what God knows and we can't see what God sees so let us trust the Lord and wait for Him to see us through. Let us hold onto the faith we profess and not mistake God's stillness for unwillingness to help us. Amen! Praise God! Rejoice in the Lord Always!

DAY 336

"For where envy and self-seeking exist, confusion and every evil thing are there."
James 3:16 NKJV

Many of us are just not satisfied with where we are in life and we yearn for what others have. We feel like we should have more; more money, bigger house and bigger car. But let us know that God has a plan for our life and He has us right where we should be, and we have what we should have. So let us be content with the blessings God has given us because He has us in our position for a reason.

Maybe He wants us to pray more, draw closer to Him, and have more faith. Whatever reason it is, if we first seek God and His wisdom, we can learn how to be content and not yearn for more. Let us wait upon the Lord to give us the desires of our heart because what God gives, lasts for eternity. Be happy about what others have and be not envious. Amen! Praise God! Rejoice in the Lord Always!

DAY 337

"This is what the LORD Almighty says: "Do not listen to what the prophets are prophesying to you; they fill you with false hopes. They speak visions from their own minds, not from the mouth of the LORD."
Jeremiah 23:16 NIV

Beware of false prophets! People are convincing others that they heard from the Lord in order for us to follow them. They want us to believe that the Lord spoke to them and told them something about us. Don't fall for it!

We must study and meditate on God's word and listen for His small voice to direct us in the way we should go. These people are using God's word for their own agenda to have people follow them, to take their money and valuables.

Let us pray daily for spiritual discernment and God will reveal to us who is truly preaching God's Word. God is not one to use people for financial gain. God wants us to bring souls to Jesus Christ. Amen! Praise God! Rejoice in the Lord Always!

Written by Delorise Reuben-McDuffie

DAY 338

"Test me, Lord, and try me, examine my heart and my mind; for I have always been mindful of your unfailing love and have lived in reliance on your faithfulness."

Psalm 26:2-3 NIV

When situations in our lives don't turn out like we expect them to, how we respond to them is what matters most. Most times, we get frustrated and confused about how to solve the problem. We first think about the worst possible outcome. But we need to always remember not to REACT but RESPOND with prayer, asking God to reveal to us how to solve the problem.

And let us try to calm ourselves enough to know that God is in control and He will always answer our prayers. Let us write this scripture on our heart so we can remember God's unfailing love and faithfulness. God never fails! Amen! Praise God! Rejoice in the Lord Always!

Written by Delorise Reuben-McDuffie

DAY 339

"Listen to this, Job; stop and consider God's wonders."

Job 37:14 NIV

Let us stop and take time out of our busy day and meditate on all the things the Lord has done for the animals, others, and us. Meditating on the wonders of the Lord can cause us to increase our faith, not to worry, and open our eyes so we can see that the Lord can do everything but fail. We will be able to recognize that God is our everything and He is all we need.

He created the heavens and the earth. He is Mighty and Powerful. He is the one that puts food on our table, clothes on our back, pays the bills each month, puts a roof over our head, heals us, and much more. We can't do what the Lord does so let us consider His wonders and let us thank Him for all that He does. Amen! Praise God! Rejoice in the Lord Always!

DAY 340

"If we are thrown into the blazing furnace, the God we serve is able to save us from it, and he will rescue us from your hand, O King."

Daniel 3:17 NIV

No matter what crisis we face, let us stand firm and remain faithful to God knowing He can rescue and save us from anything and anybody. Even when things seem like they are just getting worse and there is no end in sight, let us stand and wait upon the Lord. Let us wait by taking our mind off our troubles and begin praising God for the small victories He gives us daily.

The small victories the Lord gives us help us to increase our faith and strength so we can forge ahead and claim the bigger victories. Sometimes we don't see the small victories, but let us praise God everyday anyhow, knowing He has given us the victory.

Anytime we don't lose faith despite our circumstances, that's a victory. Anytime we resist the devil, that's a victory. Let us praise God. He gives us small victories day by day! Amen! Praise God! Rejoice in the Lord Always!

DAY 341

"In him and through faith in him we may approach God with freedom and confidence."
Ephesians 3:12 NIV

It is a privilege to be able to go to the Lord in prayer. He is on the main line waiting to hear from us. Let us know we can approach the throne of grace and speak to the Father anytime at any place. He is never too busy to hear what one of His children has to say. So whatever is going on in our life, happy or sad, let us tell it to the Lord in prayer.

Let us not be afraid. Let us not be shy because the Holy Spirit will always give us words to pray by. If we want something to change in our life, let us take it to the Lord in prayer because prayer is so powerful it can cause a chain reaction. Let us find a friend in Jesus so we can tell Him all about it. Amen! Praise God! Rejoice in the Lord Always!

DAY 342

"Therefore lay aside all filthiness and overflow of wickedness and receive with meekness the implanted word, which is able to save your souls."
James 1:21 NKJV

"God's Word is a lamp unto our feet and a light unto our path" (Psalm 119:105). It directs and guides us the way we should go. It goes before us, giving us light in all the dark places. God's Word is "active and living." It gives life to our body, soul and spirit. Many lives are being changed day by day by God's Living Word. Let us embrace God's Word and store the messages in our heart.

The Bible might have been written many years ago, but it is right for a time such as this. It is not just a book to be laid aside on the coffee table. It is a book that should be read daily for encouragement, inspiration, hope, serenity, strength, and faith. There are many blessings in the Word of God. Let us not miss out in what God has to say. Amen! Praise God! Rejoice in the Lord Always!

DAY 343

"Let no one say when he is tempted, "I am tempted by God;" for God cannot be tempted by evil, nor does He Himself tempt anyone. But each one is tempted when he is drawn away by his own desires and enticed."
James 1:13-14 NKJV

God does not tempt us. He tests us so we can be more dependent on Him and so

REJOICE: A Celebration of Life

our faith can grow. Satan tempts us with his evil desires, trying to lure us away from God. Satan does not want our life to be blessed nor does he want us to succeed. So he dresses up greed, lust, and all types of evilness to make it look enticing to us. And when we find Satan's ways enticing, we follow him and he leads us down the road to trouble, despair, and destruction.

But let us know we can get off Satan's road anytime by asking God for forgiveness and following His Word. Satan is afraid of the Word of God. So when we find ourselves tempted by him, let us fight him with our "Sword," the Word of God. Amen! Praise God! Rejoice in the Lord Always!

DAY 344

"Now may the Lord of peace himself give you peace at all times and in every way. The Lord be with all of you."
2 Thessalonians 3:16 NIV

Let us believe, have faith, hope, and trust in the Lord at all times and in all circumstances so we can have the peace only the Lord can give always within our heart, soul and spirit. Too many times, we allow our circumstances to dictate if we will have peace or not have peace. When we forget God is in control of our life and knows all about our troubles worry takes over and peace no longer resides.

Peace and worry can't reside in the same heart, soul or spirit at the same time. So let us be with God at all times so we will always be reminded and never forgetting that He is in control at all times. Let us take hold of the peace that only the Lord can give. Amen! Praise God! Rejoice in the Lord Always!

DAY 345

"When I said, "My foot is slipping," your love, O Lord supported me."
Psalm 94:18 NIV

During our most difficult times, we might feel alone but we are not alone. We can depend on the Lord our God to give us love, support, and comfort during our most trying times. God will be there to hold us up so we can stand tall through it all and not fall. We were created not to fall so when we call onto the Lord, He will build us up with strength to endure it all.

We serve an on-time God so at our weakest moments, just when we think we can't stand any more, God will show up and show out. Let us not be afraid because God will not let us fall. Thank you God for your love, grace, and mercy. Amen! Praise God! Rejoice in the Lord Always!

DAY 346

"Dear friends, do not be surprised at the painful trial you are suffering, as though something strange were happening to you."
1 Peter 4:12 NIV

We are going to go through the fire. When God wants to mold us and refine our character, He is going to take us through some rough times. He wants us to become wiser and know that with Him we can make it through anything that comes our way. He is not going to put anymore on us than we can handle, so let us know if God sends us to it, we can make it through it. So, as we go through the fire let us not "grumble" or cry "Why me?"

But let us praise the Lord and count it all joy because when He is finished with us, we are going to come out of the fire wiser, stronger, and with more faith. He is going to tell us things we never heard and show us things we have never seen before. God has a lesson and a blessing waiting for us in every

trial. Let us keep the faith. We can make it!!
Amen! Praise God! Rejoice in the Lord Always!

DAY 347

"Finally, all of you, live in harmony with one another; be sympathetic, love as brothers, be compassionate and humble."
1 Peter 3:8 NIV

Our first reaction when someone treats us unfairly is to get angry and defend ourselves. Instead, we should pray and forgive them. There's a saying, "Kill them with kindness." Try to understand that most times, people will attack us because they are hurting inside. Hurt people hurt people. Misdirected anger can be one reason people want to harm us for no reason at all.

Remember this, "It's better to understand than to be understood." God bless those who show love not hate. Most times, they will need us before we will need them. Don't let anyone steal our joy. Amen! Praise God! Rejoice in the Lord Always!

Written by Delorise Reuben-McDuffie

DAY 348

"Let the words of my mouth and the meditation of my heart be acceptable in Your sight, O Lord, my strength and my Redeemer."

Psalm 19:14 NKJV

We are not always mindful of what we say and what we think. Far too many times, we get angry and we don't speak or think the right things. And sometimes we are more interested in trying to please man and the world with our words and thoughts that we forget God is always listening. But let us think before speak.

Let us have a new way of speaking and thinking that is pleasing to the Lord. Let us go before the Lord daily in prayer and ask Him to guide our words and our thoughts so we can have a renewing of the mind. We serve an awesome God!! So let our words and thoughts be acceptable to God and not man. Amen! Praise God! Rejoice in the Lord Always!

DAY 349

"And you will be hated by all for My name's sake. But he who endures to the end shall be saved."

Mark 13:13 NKJV

It takes a whole lot of strength, endurance, and perseverance to stay on the Christian journey. Because some of our friends are not going to be happy for us when we start following Jesus Christ and going to church.

They are going to be angry and try to do everything to persuade us to come back to our old way of life. They are going to remind us about our past and how much fun we had hanging-out, but let us know with Christ the "Best is yet to come."

Let us tell our friends we are not following Christ because we are better than them. But we are following Christ because we realized that we were lost and we needed to be found. It takes a strong person to leave the crowd. Let us be strong! Amen! Praise God! Rejoice in the Lord Always!

DAY 350

"In the day of my trouble I sought the Lord; my hand was stretched out in the night without ceasing; my soul refused to be comforted."

Psalm 77:2 NKJV

When trouble comes knocking, we need someone that can really help us and comfort our soul. We don't need just any kind of help.

We need divine help; help that only the Lord can give. The Lord mighty and powerful is the only one that can turn things around for us and "make a way out of no way."

Man might try and fail; but with God, we are guaranteed a victory. For nothing is too hard for God. He is our "Ever present help in times of trouble" so let us seek the Lord when the going gets tough. We never have to stand alone because God will always stand with us and help us when we call. Amen! Praise God! Rejoice in the Lord Always!

DAY 351

"Fear not, O land; be glad and rejoice, for the Lord has done marvelous things!"
Joel 2:21 NKJV

Let us rejoice and celebrate all the marvelous things the Lord has done for us. Let us count our blessings one by one. Since the Lord has come into our life, it has never been the same. He has saved us from the pits of hell and turned our life from upside down to right side up. He has bestowed many great blessings big and small upon our family, our loved ones, and us.

It was the Lord that made it possible for us to soar above our circumstances and knock down all obstacles. Let us shout for joy and thank the Lord for all He has done, is doing, and will do. The Lord has been so great to us! Let us fear not, but continue to have faith in the Lord and His ability to do all things except fail. Amen! Praise God! Rejoice in the Lord Always!

DAY 352

"But I say to you who hear: Love your enemies, do good to those who hate you, bless those who curse you, and pray for those who spitefully use you."
Luke 6:27 NKJV

There are going to be people in the world that we encounter that hate us and use us for reasons we might never understand. But to those people who hate us and use us, let us show love to them. Let us be kind, respectful, and forgiving to them. To love God includes loving others even if they don't love us. This kind of love is not easy but it can be done with prayer and a conscious effort.

Let us remember not to fight evil with evil because God fights our battles and He punishes those who do us wrong. If we show love and forgive, we will be shown love and be forgiven! Amen! Praise God! Rejoice in the Lord Always!

DAY 353

"Listen and hear my voice; pay attention and hear what I say."
                                    Isaiah 28:23 NIV

Let us stop watching so much TV. Let us stop talking too much. Let us stop spending so much time on the computer. Let us pay attention to what the Lord has to say. God is talking to us and if we are too busy, we can't hear Him speak to us.

God has so many important things to tell us concerning our life including many important things that we never heard before that will change our life and lead us down the road to success and prosperity. God is good. He loves us and He wants to bless us.

So let us find a quiet place and hear what the Lord has to say because His plan is better than our plan. Amen! Praise God! Rejoice in the Lord Always!

DAY 354

"And the Lord will make you the head and not the tail; you shall be above only, and not be beneath, if you heed the commandments of the Lord your God, which I command you today, and are careful to observe them."
Deuteronomy 28:13 NKJV

If we want to have success all of the time instead of failure, then let us follow and obey God with all our heart and soul. This promise is impossible for man but not for God. So let us believe and not worry about how we will have success all of the time. Let us just trust God because He keeps His promises.

God is a man who cannot lie. God knows the way and He will show us the way to have success all of the time even in the midst of a storm. In order for us to achieve what God has promised, let us listen, follow, and obey. Moses, Noah and many others have already received what God has promised. Let us try God for ourselves and see. Amen! Praise God! Rejoice in the Lord Always!

DAY 355

"Woe to those who go down to Egypt for help, and rely on horses, who trust in chariots because they are many, and in horsemen because they are very strong, but who do not look to the Holy One of Israel, nor seek the Lord!"

Isaiah 31:1 NKJV

When we need help, we do not need to call on a large army, or a person of great strength; we just need to call on the Lord. The Lord Mighty and Powerful is more powerful than any army. He is and stronger than any man. He can and He will provide all the help we need. For in His Word, the Lord promises to "supply all of our needs."

So if our need is "help," the Lord will be there to supply whatever help we need. The Lord sees all, knows all, and He knows the kind of help we need even before we do. No matter how big or how strong, no man can do what the Lord does! Let us trust in the Lord and allow Him to be our helper when we call. Amen! Praise God! Rejoice in the Lord Always!

DAY 356

"And the prayer of faith will save the sick, and the Lord will raise him up."
James 5:15a NKJV

Let us know God is a healer. He is our Chief Physician! He heals our body, soul, and spirit. So when a loved one, family member, or an enemy among us is sick let us pray for their recovery. Let us not make kneeling before the Lord in prayer our last resort when all else fails. Instead, it should be our first choice because the Father is our greatest resource. And the Father is the only one who can make the sick whole again.

Let us remember that when we pray, we need to have faith that God can heal and that He hears us, He will answer us, and that His "will" will be done. Sometimes God will only heal the soul and spirit. We might not understand why, but let us know He has a reason for everything. When we go before God in prayer, He gives us strength to withstand the pressure from any storm. Let us pray and believe! Amen! Praise God! Rejoice in the Lord Always!

DAY 357

"Ah, Sovereign Lord, you have made the heavens and the earth by your great power and outstretched arm. Nothing is too hard for you."

Jeremiah 32:17 NIV

There is "Nothing too hard for God!" Let us remind ourselves of that scripture when we begin to doubt God's ability to give us what we prayed, or to be the head of our life, or to solve our problems. God's ways and thoughts are much higher than are ours. God orchestrates everything in heaven and here on earth, and He is everywhere.

God can do everything we can't do, so let us not put a limit on what He can do. Let us trust God to do what He says He will do and to solve all of our problems. He is superior in power, strength, wisdom, knowledge...and in all things. God is Sovereign. Let us trust and depend on Him! Amen! Praise God! Rejoice in the Lord Always!

DAY 358

"This is how the birth of Jesus Christ came about: His mother Mary was pledged to be married to Joseph, but before they came together, she was found to be with child through the Holy Spirit."

Matthew 1:18-19 NIV

The birth of Jesus Christ made all the difference for us. Thank you God for giving us your Only begotten Son so that we may have a chance of a new life through the birth of your Son, Jesus Christ. Because Jesus lives, we can now begin a new life with a new way of thinking, walking, and talking, leaving our past life behind us.

We no longer have to worry about yesterday, today or tomorrow because Jesus lives, and He now holds the key to our future. We can now replace our fear with faith in Jesus Christ and have more hope, joy, and serenity. "Because He lives, we can face tomorrow." Amen! Praise God! Rejoice in the Lord Always!

DAY 359

"The Word became flesh and made his dwelling among us. We have seen His glory, the glory of the One and Only, who came from the Father, full of grace and truth."
John 1:14 NIV

When Christ was born, God became a man who lived here on earth. Jesus is that man. He is both God and man. We serve a Triune God who is the Father, the Son, and the Holy Spirit. Jesus came into this world to save us and give us life.

John 10:10 Jesus says, "I have come that they may have life, and that they may have it more abundantly." Thanks to Jesus, we can know the fullness of God's grace, mercy, love, and forgiveness. Jesus reveals God's glory to us through the miracles He performs and by his death and resurrection.

Therefore, let us celebrate the birth of Jesus Christ with praise and worship, forgiveness, love, and giving to those in need. Amen! Praise God! Rejoice in the Lord Always!

DAY 360

"The tongue has the power of life and death, and those who love it will eat its fruit."
                    Proverbs 18:21 NIV

The words we speak matter; they can either hurt or heal. So let us encourage others and ourselves with the words that we speak. There is so much depression, despair and hopelessness in this world today that sometimes we need to speak words that stir up and initiate love, kindness, serenity and inspiration. We have the power within us to speak life or death let us chose words that give life.

Let us inspire and promote self-confidence to others and ourselves. When we lift up others and ourselves, it can lead to one having more faith, hope and joy. Let us speak the same words that we want to hear from others. Amen! Praise God! Rejoice in the Lord Always!

DAY 361

"For the Lord your God is the one who goes with you to fight for you against your enemies to give you victory."

Deuteronomy 20:4 NIV

The victory will always be ours in all circumstances, if we believe, trust and call on God our Father in our time of battle against our enemies. Our enemies are not always people, but also our trials, tribulations, burdens, dark days, disappointments, illness, hurt, pain; anything and everything we have to battle and overcome.

The Lord tells us not to be afraid and not to worry because He is the one that will fight for us. 2 Chronicles 20:15b says "For the battle is not yours, but God's. So let us call on the Lord and allow Him to fight all of our battles, because there is "Nobody Greater." We can't always win but the Lord can! Trust Him! Amen! Praise God! Rejoice in the Lord Always!

DAY 362

"Oh, magnify the Lord with me, and let us exalt His name together."
Psalm 34:3 NKJV

Let us lift up the name of Jesus and magnify Him! "Let every knee bow and every tongue confess that Jesus Christ is Lord." God highly exalted Jesus and gave Him the name which is above all another names. There is no other person like Jesus. He is the one and only "Great I am." His sandals, we cannot wear.

Oh, let us magnify the Lord and remember the many ways He has been there for us. By His grace and mercy, the Lord has kept us and brought us through many nights. He is our Shepherd and we are His sheep. And a shepherd knows and takes care of his sheep.

It is a blessing just to know the Lord. The Lord is good to all who love and seek Him with all of their heart, soul and mind. Let everyone that has breath magnify the Lord! Hallelujah! Amen! Praise God! Rejoice in the Lord Always!

DAY 363

"Heal me, O Lord, and I shall be healed; save me, and I shall be saved, for you are my praise."

Jeremiah 17:14 NJKV

We can trust, depend on and have faith in the Lord because He will do what He promises He will do. When the Lord makes us a promise, we can count on Him to deliver on that promise.

No one can stop the Lord from delivering on His promise or change what He has done because He is the greatness, and His "will" will always be done. We just need to be patient and wait on the Lord to make good on His promise. When we don't wait, we don't get what the Lord has for us.

God promised to deliver the Israelites out of Egypt and He delivered them out of Egypt. So when we ask the Lord to heal us, let us know we shall be healed. When we ask the Lord to save us, let us know we shall be saved. Whatever we ask in the "Name of the Lord," let us know we shall receive. Have Faith! Amen! Praise God! Rejoice in the Lord Always!

DAY 364

"He has delivered us from the power of darkness and conveyed us into the kingdom of the Son of His love, in whom we have redemption through His blood, the forgiveness of sins."

Colossians 1:13-14 NKJV

The chains have been broken. We do not have to be a slave to sin any longer. Satan no longer has a hold on us. We can now walk away from Satan and our past sins and walk into the life God has planned for us.

Our freedom has been brought by the blood of Jesus Christ, the Son of God. Hallelujah!! Jesus shed His blood for you and I so that we might have the right to the "tree of life." Jesus who is without sin took on the sins of the world.

Through His suffering and death, Jesus bore the punishment for our sins. He brought us peace with God and He healed our spirit. Now let us walk out of the darkness and into the beautiful light. Amen! Praise God! Rejoice in the Lord Always!

DAY 365

"Rejoice in the Lord Always. Again I will say, rejoice!"

Philippians 4:4 NKJV

Let us praise our way through the storm. Let us not allow our circumstances to steal our joy, rob us of our inner peace, and cause us to lose hope or faith. When a crisis comes our way, it is easy for us to get sad, discouraged, hopeless, and fearful of the unknown. But all of that can be changed. We can have faith, joy, hope and peace while going through a crisis if we just keep our mind on the Lord.

Let us keep our mind on the Lord and know trouble don't last forever because at any moment the Lord is going to turn our circumstances around. The Lord is in full control. He knows all about our troubles and He will give us the victory. So let us give the Lord the highest praise "Hallelujah" all the way through the storm. Amen! Praise God! Rejoice in the Lord Always!

About the Author

Renee Lindsay-Thompson was born in New York City, New York. Her early childhood was spent in the Bronx and she later moved to Newburgh, NY.

Her educational experience includes an A.S. Degree in Business Administration. Further professional education includes a Diploma as Licensed Practical Nurse and A.A.S. Degree as Registered Nurse.

As a Licensed Practical Nurse, Renee managed several employees, doctor's offices and clinical areas. She has also received multiple awards and recognition for customer service. However, Renee's physical disability prevented her from continuing in her nursing career as a Registered Nurse.

Renee was ordained a Deacon at Powerhouse Church of Christ, New York, NY. She later attended Mt. Carmel Church of Christ Disciples of Christ in Newburgh, NY. After moving to Atlanta, she joined Greenforest Community Baptist Church in Decatur, Georgia.

Her hobbies are swimming, collecting angels, and sitting on the beach.

Renee is the Founder/President of Rejoice: A Celebration of Life, a 2010 new start-up company with a mission of spreading the Word of God through Daily Inspirational Messages.

Renee Lindsay-Thompson is married to Robert Thompson and has a daughter, Lindsay Randolph.

Daily Meditations

SCRIPTURAL INDEX

Isa. 40:11 KJV	39	Jer. 10:23 NIV	134
Isa. 40:29 NKJV	280	Jer. 17:7-8 NIV	1
Isa. 40:31 NIV	129	Jer. 17:14 NJKV	320
Isa. 41:9 NIV	34	Jer. 23:16 NIV	296
Isa. 41:10b NKJV	131	Jer. 29:11 NIV	131
Isa. 43:1-3 NKJV	73	Jer. 32:17 NIV	314
Isa. 43:10b-11,13b NIV	161	Job 22:21 NIV	250
Isa. 43:16 KJV	151	Job 22:27 NIV	181
Isa. 43:18-19A NIV	150	Job 23:10b NKJV	246
Isa. 45:18-19 NIV	2	Job 27:6 NIV	209
Isa. 46:4 NIV	270	Job 36:15 NIV	153
Isa. 46:11 NIV	20	Job 37:14 NIV	298
Isa. 48:10 NKJV	204	Joel 2:21 NKJV	308
Isa. 54:17 KJV	225	John 1:14 NIV	316
Isa. 55:6 NKJV	286	John 1:16 NIV	39
Isa. 63:9 NIV	145	John 3:30 NKJV	146
Jam. 1:4 NKJV	110	John 5:5 NKJV	148
Jam. 1:6-8 NKJV	105	John 6:35 NKJV	15
Jam. 1:12 NKJV	111	John 8:32 NIV	132
Jam. 1:13-14 NKJV	301	John 9:1-3 NKJV	170
Jam. 1:16-17 NIV	264	John 10:10 NKJV	128
John 11:27 NKJV	235	Luke 17:12-17 NKJV	75
John 11:35 NKJV	237	Luke 18:1 NIV	35
John 12:13 NIV	137	Luke 19:45-46 NIV	121

REJOICE: A Celebration of Life

Daily Meditations

Pro. 4:11-12 NIV	261	Psa. 46:10 NKJV	277
Pro. 15:1 NKJV	103	Psa. 51:2,10 NKJV	119
Pro. 18:21 NIV	317	Psa. 51:17 NIV	182
Pro. 24:3-4 NKJV	37	Psa. 55:22 NIV	6
Pro. 26:22 KJV	74	Psa. 56:3 NKJV	144
Psa. 3:2 NIV	122	Psa. 62:2 NIV	12
Psa. 5:2 NKJV	277	Psa. 62:8 NIV	168
Psa. 5:11a NIV	178	Psa. 68:19 NIV	83
Psa. 16:11 NKJV	85	Psa. 73:26 NIV	179
Psa. 18:2 NKJV	252	Psa. 77:2 NKJV	307
Psa. 19:14 NKJV	306	Psa. 139:17-18 NIV	176
Psa. 83:1 NIV	294	Psa. 138:7 NIV	288
Psa. 90:17 NIV	97	Psa. 138:8 NIV	231
Psa. 91:1-2 NIV	112	Psa. 139:7-10 NIV	69
Psa. 91:9-12 NIV	199	Psa. 139:13-14 NIV	194
Psa. 91:14-16 NIV	5	Psa. 139:16 NIV	290
Psa. 92:1-2, 4 NIV	125	Psa. 143:5 NKJV	53
Psa. 94:18 NIV	303	Psa. 147:3 NKJV	216
Psa. 95:1-2 NKJV	272	Psa. 148:1,5,13 NKJV	114
Psa. 95:1, 3 NKJV	35	Psa. 150 1-2, 8 NKJV	95
Psa. 95:2 NKJV	289	Rom. 3:23 NKJV	16
Psa. 95:6-7 NIV	143	Rom. 8:28 NKJV	30
Psa. 100:4 NIV	12	Rom. 8:31 NIV	21
Psa. 100:5 NIV	102	Rom. 8:35 NIV	22

REJOICE: A Celebration of Life

Made in the USA
Charleston, SC
25 March 2013